Speaking the Truth in Love

ALSO BY J. PHILIP WOGAMAN

Methodism's Challenge in Race Relations (1960)

Protestant Faith and Religious Liberty (1967)

Guaranteed Annual Income: The Moral Issues (1968)

The Population Crisis and Moral Responsibility (editor; 1973)

A Christian Method of Moral Judgment (1976)

The Great Economic Debate: An Ethical Analysis (1977)

Quality of Life in a Global Society (with Paul McCleary; 1978)

Faith and Fragmentation: Christianity for a New Age (1985)

Economics and Ethics: A Christian Inquiry (1986)

Christian Perspectives on Politics (1988)

Christian Moral Judgment (1989)

Making Moral Decisions (1991)

Christian Ethics: A Historical Introduction (1993)

To Serve the Present Age:
The Gifts and Promise of United Methodism (1995)

Readings in Christian Ethics: A Historical Sourcebook
(editor, with Douglas M. Strong; 1996)

Speaking the Truth in Love

Prophetic Preaching to a Broken World

J. PHILIP WOGAMAN

Westminster John Knox Press
Louisville, Kentucky

Scripture quotations, unless otherwise noted, are from the New Revised Standard Version of the Bible, copyright © 1989 by the Division of Christian Education of the National Council of the Churches of Christ in the U.S.A., and are used by permission.

Book design by Jennifer K. Cox
Cover design by Kim Wohlenhaus

Cover illustration: Peaceable Kingdom, © *1994 by John August Swanson*
Serigraph 30" by 22 1/2"
    Los Angeles artist John August Swanson is noted for his finely detailed, brilliantly colored biblical pieces. His works are found in the Smithsonian Institution's National Museum of American History, London's Tate Gallery, the Vatican Museum's Collection of Modern Religious Art, and The Bibliothèque Nationale, Paris. Represented by the Bergsma Gallery, Grand Rapids, Michigan, (616) 458-1776.
    Full-color posters and cards of Mr. Swanson's work are available from the National Association of Hispanic Elderly. Benefits go to its programs of employment of seniors and to housing low-income seniors. For information, contact National Association of Hispanic Elderly, 234 East Colorado Blvd., Suite 300, Pasadena, CA 91101, (626) 564-1988.

First edition
Published by Westminster John Knox Press
Louisville, Kentucky

This book is printed on acid-free paper that meets the American National Standards Institute Z39.48 standard. ∞

PRINTED IN THE UNITED STATES OF AMERICA
98 99 00 01 02 03 04 05 06 07 — 10 9 8 7 6 5 4 3 2 1

Library of Congress Cataloging-in-Publication Data

Wogaman, J. Philip.
    Speaking the truth in love : prophetic preaching to a broken world /
J. Philip Wogaman. — 1st ed.
        p.   cm.
    Includes bibliographical references.
    ISBN 0-664-25774-7 (alk. paper)
    1. Preaching   2. Sociology, Christian—Sermons.   3. United
Methodist Church (U.S.)—Sermons.   4. Sermons, American.   I. Title.
BV4235.S6W64   1998
251—dc21   98-19219

Dedicated, with affection, to my grandchildren

Carolyn Martha
John Philip, II
Carrie Adelaide
Paul Joseph, Jr.

Contents

Preface

In 1992, after twenty-six years as a seminary professor of Christian ethics, I was asked to become pastor of a downtown church in the nation's capital. After all those years of encouraging seminary students to address the hard issues of the day in their sermons, the time had come to put up or shut up. (My wife, on the other hand, simply observed that it had taken me longer to get out of seminary than most students.) I wondered, perhaps naively, whether I could translate my teaching of Christian ethics into a serious dialogue with a very diverse congregation that included some people of modest economic and educational status and others with enormous influence in the public life of the nation. I had preached often enough through the years as a seminary professor, but not on a sustained basis to the same congregation.

With this move I was to learn a lot more about the spiritual needs that cut across all lines of status and power. I was to learn more about what it means to love a congregation full of people and to try to reach their hearts and minds through that love. I was to share their alternating high moments and low moments and to see, in new ways, how people's spiritual lives are interwoven with moral and theological issues.

I have found that my years of teaching are relevant to pastoral ministry, and this book is an effort to contribute something out of that intersection between Christian ethics and preaching. It is born out of my great commitment both to preaching and to Christian ethics and from the realization that neither amounts to much if detached from the deep resources of Christian faith.

Part I of this volume contains my reflections on prophetic preaching. The first three chapters reflect on the meaning of "prophetic" (including why it is not always or necessarily controversial) and the theological and pastoral setting of prophetic preaching. I am convinced that such preaching must be solidly grounded biblically and theologically and that it must be an expression of a broader pastoral ministry. Chapter 4 is a reminder that preaching is a part of the broader worship life of the church. Chapters 5 through 7 deal with the connections to be made between theology and life experience in our preaching. How concrete and specific should we be in "naming the evils" and identifying the most promising solutions to the moral problems of our age? How do particular faith themes or doctrines help illuminate the moral landscape? And what broad perspectives should guide us in preaching about politics, economics, race and ethnic relations, and family life? (Here I am drawing upon a lifetime of study of Christian social ethics, now with an eye toward preaching.) Chapters 8 and 9 discuss the arts of prophetic preaching and the traps to be avoided. In the last chapter of Part I, I consider what is to be learned from the inevitable criticism—and how we can respond creatively and not too defensively.

These chapters are not, of course, to be considered a definitive manual on preaching! Most preachers do not rely on any one source for that, any more than they copy the methods and style of any one preaching mentor. Nevertheless, I hope this discussion will contribute to the mix of resources for those who take preaching, especially prophetic preaching, seriously.

Part II is made up of my own sermons. I publish them here, ever mindful of Dr. Martin Luther King's observation that sermons are meant to be heard and not read but also with the conviction that we can learn from reading one another's work. I am aware that it may seem pretentious to present a number of sermons in a book on prophetic preaching, as though these model what prophetic sermons ought to be. I do not offer them here in that spirit at all. But having written *about* prophetic preaching, it seems only fair to expose a sampling of my own sermons to view—prefaced in each case by a few comments about the setting, my intentions, and the particular problems being addressed.

Early in my ministry at Foundry Church, I was invited to reflect on prophetic preaching in a lecture to the American Academy of Homiletics. That got this project started. I told the assembled professors of preaching that *they* were the most intimidating audience I had had to face! But they were a gracious lot, and they reminded me that in the end we are all trying to help one another be better preachers. I have subsequently taught classes on prophetic preaching at Wesley Theological Seminary in Washington and at the Graduate Theological Union in Berkeley. I am particularly grateful to the nine students who met regularly with me at Wesley in the fall of 1997, hearing portions of this manuscript and commenting helpfully on it, just as I sought to be helpful in responding to their practice sermons. So, my thanks to Margaret E. Bryant, Lillie Wallace Gray, Shelby M. Haggray, Susan M. Hallager, Ronald Hemphill, Travis D. Knoll, Sherrin Marshall, Maleia A. Rust, and Bradford C. Schoeberle. Late in the process of preparing the volume, I presented a substantial portion of Part I as the annual Heck Lectures at the United Theological Seminary, Dayton, Ohio. The response of that audience was both useful and encouraging. Professor William B. McClain and the Rev. William A. Holmes each read the entire manuscript and offered useful advice. While I am grateful to all the people who have helped make this a better book, I do not hold them responsible for remaining mistakes and limitations.

The congregation of Foundry United Methodist Church has been a constant source of encouragement and helpful criticism. All of the sermons in Part II were preached at this church. This congregation helps me remember that preaching is never a purely individualistic enterprise. At every stage of preparation and delivery, the people participate far more fully than they can ever know. It is a great privilege to be asked to preach to any congregation, but I can think of no church where I would rather preach than this one.

Stephanie Egnotovich, managing editor of Westminster John Knox Press, provided indispensable editorial advice and correc-

Preface

tion. I am grateful to Sally Mathews and Sherie Koob for important secretarial assistance with this project. And I remain ever grateful to my wife, Carolyn, easily the best critic and source of encouragement of my preaching.

PART I

REFLECTIONS
ON PROPHETIC PREACHING

one

What Is Prophetic Preaching?

To some, the word "prophetic" means accuracy in predicting future events. To others, the term conjures up images of angry figures like Amos and John the Baptist, denouncing the sins and injustices of the powerful. Many think of it as adversarial and controversial. People may think of prophets as tending toward self-righteousness, even as they call attention to unpleasant truths. The prophetic is frequently contrasted with the "pastoral" or the "priestly" or the "evangelical." Thus, the prophetic can be seen as embodying something of the "works of the law" that the apostle Paul contrasted with faith and grace: A prophet busily tells people what they ought to do to make themselves acceptable to God, while an evangelist proclaims that they can trust in God's redeeming grace through faith in the Lord Jesus Christ. A pastor, meanwhile, is taken to be one who concentrates on helping people with their personal problems, and a priest emphasizes the worship life of a community of faith.

I wish to distance myself from such understandings of the word, at least for the purposes of this book. To be prophetic is not necessarily to be adversarial, or even controversial. The word in its Greek form refers to one who speaks in behalf of another. In Hebrew tradition, a prophet is one who speaks for God—or at least claims to, for some came to be seen as false prophets.

What does it mean to speak for God? Often, in the Hebrew scriptures, the message is delivered as though it was conveyed to the prophet in very explicit language and is meant to go through the prophet to the people: "Thus says the Lord." God has spoken directly to the prophet, and the people are admonished to take heed. But one does not have to assume any kind of mechanical transmission of the message from God to the prophet to get the main point: The prophet has a singular grasp of what God intends. Through the prophet the people have a window into the reality of God and how the reality of God can shape and direct their existence. A portion of James Russell Lowell's poem "Columbus," though in a different context, is suggestive:

> For I believed the poets; it is they
> Who utter wisdom from the central deep,
> And, listening to the inner flow of things,
> Speak to the age out of eternity.[1]

This is exactly the job description of the prophet. To speak for another is to grasp, first, the mind of the other. A prophetic preacher cannot claim to know the whole mind of God—though some prophets may have thought they did. But genuinely prophetic preaching draws people into the reality of God in such a way that they cannot any longer be content with conventional wisdom and superficial existence.

Prophetic preaching is absolutely essential. The church, as religious institution, is constantly pressed into the service of social conventions and existing powers. Sometimes the prevailing culture and powers are, on the whole, good and just. Even so, if the church is only a conforming institution, its power to deepen the lives of its people and to influence the culture is very limited. It cannot really be the church that it has always been called to be. The problem is all the more urgent in a climate of oppression and corruption, when a sharply challenging voice must be heard. The Russian Orthodox Church, for instance, was ill equipped to confront the perils of bolshevism because it was so deeply compromised by its relationship with the previous czarist regime—a problem to be repeated by the more evangelical Protestant churches of Cuba, which had no serious tradition of prophetic thought and moved quickly from a more individualistic pietism into an uncritical welcoming of the new Marxist order. The church of the "German Christians" easily accommodated itself to the Nazi regime, with theological interpretations of the führer principle and the new order. A handful of courageous preachers, such as Martin Niemöller, paid a serious price for standing against this in the pulpit. The confessing church of Dietrich Bonhoeffer, though small in numbers, gave visual embodiment to the prophetic impulse as it sought to counter the idolatries and acculturations of mainstream Christians during the Nazi era.

Everywhere such illustrations leap to mind, for everywhere the church is drawn toward a role of social reinforcement. This is as true in the United States as anywhere else. Christian support for slavery, though largely regional, was serious and deep. A whole mythology was developed in the 1830s and 1840s to justify the institution on the basis of Noah's drunken curse against Ham and his son Canaan (in Genesis 9), along with New Testament admonitions to slaves to obey their masters. Even in the northern states, the voices of Christian abolitionists were criticized for disturbing the fragile peace. At other times the Christian pulpit has served to demonize the nation's enemies. Ray Abrams, in his 1933 book *Preachers Present Arms*,[2] presents fascinating excerpts from sermons preached during World War I. Germans were portrayed in the most inhuman terms; the cause of the United States and its allies in the "war to end wars" was set forth as a holy crusade. Similarly, many pulpits of the Cold War era demonized the "godless Communists" and helped lay the cultural foundation that accepted the need to ready ourselves for nuclear war.

It is always easier in retrospect to see the captivity and shortsightedness of a culturally accommodating church. Today we *know* that slavery is wrong, just as we can better perceive the gray areas of involvement in World War I and the ambiguities of the Cold War. It is easier for people now to see that the destruction caused by nuclear war would have been disproportionate to any good it might have served, but for fifty years this reasoning was not so clear. Racism continues to be a cultural force in this country, but seldom does one see or hear it defended theologically. We are also a good deal clearer that women are equal to men. Today we honor the pioneers of the faith who saw and announced that truth at the time it was most needed and most beleaguered. Later generations build the monuments to the prophets; at the time they speak, they are stoned!

It is perhaps inevitable that people should push religion toward cultural accommodation. Religion gives expression to our ultimate values—the God or gods we worship. The culture that forms us and within which we live is a whole tapestry of specific and sometimes conflicting values. Inevitably we seek support for our lesser values in the deeper religious commitments that provide ultimate meaning to us. Life in any culture is intolerable when our way of life is not consonant with our ultimate beliefs. We try to shape and bend our faith to accommodate our culture. There is generally more "Christ of culture," in H. Richard Niebuhr's phrase, than "Christ transforming culture."

Still, the relationship between faith and culture is always more subtle and complex than I have suggested. The pressure toward cultural conformity is great. But religious faith also has enormous power to create change. When people believe deeply and are deeply committed to their beliefs, the tensions between their beliefs and their social existence become intolerable. It is then that people are most motivated to change their own life patterns, along with the social institutions of which they are a part. So there is a tension between cultural accommodation and the impulse to change.

The preacher is in a unique position to help focus the life of the church more clearly, while also speaking beyond the church to the wider world. He or she speaks to people in the context of worship about the meaning and implications of what is most important to them. But the preacher speaks, also, implicitly, in the context of the congregation's existence in the world. The pulpit is at the intersection of faith and culture, where people are nourished in the faith and invited to think about their values and practices in its light. To occupy the pulpit is a great privilege. It is a privilege that can be abused, either by failing to take our responsibility seriously enough or by using it manipulatively.

But for a preacher who takes it seriously, this privilege can make a large difference. The very fact that prophetic preaching sometimes encounters vigorous opposition should tell us something. People do not get exercised about events that do not matter to them! When there is a real conflict between what we believe about God and the life patterns to which we are also committed, it is no wonder that we want to avoid the resulting tension. No wonder the prophet Micah was admonished, "Do not preach . . . one should not preach of such things" (Micah 2:6). How many faithful preachers, before and after Micah, have heard almost exactly those words! If it is uncomfortable for people to hear preaching that exposes the conflict between faith and practice, it can be even more uncomfortable for the preacher who feels called to do the exposing. Often people will blame the messenger in order to resist the message.

But because prophetic preaching means bringing the light of the gospel to bear upon all aspects of human existence, it will inevitably lead to some conflict, some controversy. For human existence is riddled with conflict. Contemporary preachers are not exempt from responses similar to those Jesus had to face. Despite bringing a gospel that is altogether framed in love, Jesus had to face intense opposition. There is no evidence that Jesus sought controversy for its own sake, but the gospel he bore made argument impossible to escape. Clearly, prophetic preaching often is controversial, for it must frequently challenge settled ways of thinking and living with a deeper truth.

But is prophetic preaching *necessarily* controversial? No, not always. Consider Jesus again: His stern words of criticism for self-righteous religious leaders and for King Herod were doubtless intended to sharpen issues. But what about his words, spoken to the humble people of the land? "You are the salt of the earth. . . . You are the light of the world . . . let your light shine before others, so that they may see your good works and give glory to your Father in heaven." Spoken to poor people of low self-esteem, this was revolutionary language. It said, in effect, Get ahold of yourselves; you really matter to God. That is a genuinely prophetic word.

Whenever preachers have spoken to neglected, oppressed people, the word of their liberation and salvation challenges their settled loathing of themselves. Is this controversial? Sometimes it is indeed controversial, among those who wish to keep the oppressed under control. Sometimes, unfortunately, it can also be controversial among the disinherited themselves, who fear the consequences of change more than the possibilities of liberation. But it really is good news to be told that God cares a lot about you and has a real place for you in the beloved community that is to come. Not all slaves welcome the prospect of liberation, but surely most do. Not all victims of racism, having absorbed the doctrine of their own inferiority, welcome a message of their total human value, but surely most do. Not all women, after millennia of subordinate status, welcome genuine equality, but more do than most men can imagine! To be told that your life is of great value to God is deeply prophetic. Sometimes, indeed, the message is controversial, but not necessarily. It is not controversial among those who welcome the word of their value to God and the message of their liberation.

Most pastors have experienced those moments, either in the privacy of a counseling session or in the pulpit, when they have looked people in the eye and pleaded with them to see their human value and their possibilities: Don't sell yourself short! Don't throw your life away! The message may be stern, even angry. But it is based on the strongest possible affirmation of the personhood and value of those to whom it is addressed.

Even a stern rebuke to oppressors can be framed as good news to them. Racists, for example, have devalued themselves by treating superficial physical characteristics as most important in their humanity. In that sense, the first victim of racism is the racist, because to believe in racism is to believe that you have no real value as a human being. Cannot the same be said about those who cling to wealth in the face of poverty or to those who have defined their own lives in terms of power and prestige? Is it not good news to learn that life is more than that? "Do not store up for yourselves treasures on earth, where moth and rust consume and where thieves break in and steal." How good to know that moth and rust and thieves do not have the last word concerning our value and that our worth, based upon God's love, is not so perishable. Wealth, power, and prestige, when sought for their own sake and as the main purpose in life, are finally empty. At best, they are consolation prizes for those who have lost the main thing. It is good news to come to know that life really is more than this.

Thus, even the gospel as judgment is first the gospel as good news. The gospel as judgment means helping people see how tragic and unnecessary it is to live selfishly rather than for others. We can speak of divine judgment in this way insofar as we understand this to be a world in which God has the last word—and where that word ultimately is the word of grace. While the word of grace often must ignite controversy, it is also in the end the only basis upon which controversy can be resolved. The prophet, as God's ambassador, is called to preach that word with courage, but also with winsome grace.

The world's foremost evangelist, Rev. Billy Graham, is not best known for the prophetic content of his message. Indeed, he once contrasted the role of being an Old Testament prophet to that of a New Testament evangelist while identifying himself as the latter and not the former. But I once witnessed a very prophetic moment in his preaching career. The occasion was his evangelistic crusade in my home city, Washington, D.C. Night after night, very large crowds flocked to Washington's Convention Center to hear the famous preacher. One night—the night I had chosen to go—was designated as military night. Thousands of military personnel and veterans were on hand, and the early part of the program was heavy with patriotic music and rhetoric. This, I decided, was going to be a real exercise in civil religion. A paraplegic Vietnam veteran was brought forward for one of the preliminary addresses. The speech was partly his religious testimonial, but it was also a judgmental attack on the Soviet Union and our need to be prepared for total war if necessary. He was repeatedly interrupted with applause. Following this speech, well before the scheduled time for his sermon, Dr. Graham went to the podium to comment. He began by commending the veteran for his courage in dealing with his injuries and acknowledging the importance of the military. But then he spoke of his personal experiences in the Soviet Union, visiting with and preaching to many thousands of fellow Christians. He could not imagine, he said, the horror of nuclear war in which we would be responsible for killing those people and the rest of God's children on the other side of the Iron Curtain. The words were expressed with gentleness and grace. Clearly, not many had come expecting to hear such sentiments from the famous evangelist. Applause was muted. I did not, myself, agree with everything he had to say in his subsequent sermon. But as the evening drew to a close, it was clear to me that I had been in the presence of one who had indeed managed to combine the vocations of New Testament evangelist and Old Testament prophet, and this was exactly the word of God for that moment.

One way or another, it must be the vocation of every preacher to be both prophet and evangelist, and pastor as well.

two

Why Prophetic Preaching Must Be Theological

There is a cardinal rule of effective communication, well known to public speakers, advertisers, politicians, and everybody else who wishes to influence the opinions of others: One must build upon values *already held* by the intended audience. People's values can be changed, to be sure, but to communicate effectively one must begin from values that are already present. For instance, American advertisers often use young models to sell merchandise because youth is highly prized in our culture. (In other cultures it might be smarter for advertisers to associate their product with the wisdom of age.) Or competitive values will often speak more appealingly to men, while relational values are more likely to gain a response from women.

A classic prophetic illustration of this principle is the opening speech in Amos (chapters 1 and 2) in which he appeals to the prejudices of his listeners by criticizing the sins of Israel's enemies—Damascus, Gaza, Tyre, Edom, the Ammonites, Moab—sharply condemning the injustices and atrocities of each. Amos would not have gotten an argument about any of that; he was voicing the prejudices of his audience and, whether those views were well-founded or not, his audience would have agreed with him. Then, once he established this rapport, Amos homed in on Judah, the sister kingdom, "led astray by the same lies after which their ancestors walked." And then came the real target—"Thus says the Lord: For three transgressions of Israel, and for four, I will not revoke the punishment; because they sell the righteous for silver, and the needy for a pair of sandals—they who trample the head of the poor into the dust of the earth"—followed by a litany of other sins and injustices of the people he was addressing.

Was that effective speech? He certainly had everyone's attention! We know almost nothing of the specific occasion or the exact effects; we do know that Amos had impact, at least enough to have his words become a part of the sacred canon of Hebrew scripture.

When we preach today, how do we establish that kind of contact and have that kind of impact with the audience? First of all, no matter the congregation, we had better be grounded in the Bible. How important is that? From the purely rhetorical standpoint, suppose a speaker wanted to connect with a Muslim audience. Wouldn't it be important to know something of the Qur'an and the culture of the land in which the people were located? That would make sense even if one were a Christian missionary desirous of converting the Muslims. For most Christians, the Bible is the central repository of teaching. One must be biblical in some recognizable sense in order to be effective. In most churches, one must be biblical in some sense even to get a hearing.

Of course, the preacher's concern is more than getting a hearing or being effective. The concern is to speak the word of God, to be a spokesperson for God, to "speak to the age out of eternity," as Lowell wrote. That is an even deeper reason to preach out of the Bible, for it is in the Bible that we meet most directly the story, the history and traditions, of our faith. Here is the main account of how our faith came to be, the effect it had upon those to whom it came, the meanings they ascribed to it. The faith itself entails recognition that God *continues* to work in the lives of people. The meaning of the biblical narrative has been debated by Christian thinkers throughout subsequent history, but it is difficult to imagine Christian preaching that is not in a very basic way "biblical."

But what does it mean to preach biblically? For some, it is to take the whole Bible as literal truth and to consider that its words are, quite tangibly, the very words of God. When the Bible is referred to as the "Word of God," sometimes this is what is intended. By that standard, preaching that repeated and elaborated any part of scripture would be "prophetic," for in this way the preacher would quite literally be God's spokesperson, reiterating God's own words. But is the Bible the word of God in that sense? Surely the Bible is "inspired" by God—that is, taken as a whole, the writers of the Bible were in God's Spirit. Still, there are good reasons why a preacher should not approach the Bible in so simple a way. First, we do not even have the original words as set down by the writers of the Bible. No doubt what we have, even in translation, is close to the original. But we have long since lost the exact words. At a deeper level, the New Testament identifies *Christ* as the "Word of God," not the written pages. "[T]he Word [*Logos*] became flesh and lived among us, and we have seen his glory, the glory as of a father's only son, full of grace and truth" (John 1:14). The written words are a testimony to God's engagement with human history, especially through Jesus Christ. So Jesus Christ provides us with the standard by which to measure scripture. The God who is revealed in Christ is the one who is at work throughout human history, even when dimly perceived or misunderstood by people.

The real problem with biblical literalism is that it offers us only a unidimensional Bible—all on one level, all to be treated equally as "God's holy word." Such a Bible forces us to place the trivial alongside the profound, to take the obviously culture-bound and the historically relative portions of scripture as equally the voice of God. Can we regard Paul's comment, "Does not nature itself teach you that if a man wears long hair, it is degrading to him, but if a woman has long hair, it is her glory?"(1 Cor. 11:14–15), as being on the same level as his words "There is no longer Jew or Greek, there is no longer slave or free, there is no longer male and female; for all of you are one in Christ Jesus" (Gal. 3:28)?

The net effect of treating all biblical teaching as being on the same level is, I am afraid, to miss the true voice of God. The mechanical way in which scripture is so often handled by fundamentalist preachers underscores the point. How often it is a slinging of texts at the listener, as though the verbal acceptance would provide salvation. But such a mechanical use of the Bible actually obscures the more important teachings. A bit of repartee by a preacher during the fundamentalist controversy of the early decades of the twentieth century makes the point. Asked whether he took the Bible literally, this preacher replied, "I do not take it literally; I take it *seriously*."

How in our preaching are we to take the Bible seriously and thus struggle with the message God would have us bring? There is no way around it: A preacher must also be a theologian! A preacher must struggle with the *meaning* of the faith. Preeminently that means exploring the meaning of the revelation of God through scripture. Partly this entails recognizing that some parts of scripture are much deeper than other parts and engaging in a lifelong process of sorting it all out. Partly this requires us to face anew—at least weekly!—our fallibility. How are we to know what is *really* the truth about God? The answer is, we aren't. At least we aren't ever going to have the *whole* truth; even the truth we do have is likely to be mixed with errors derived from our human limitations. I am not sure whether that is good or bad. It would be nice to have all truth securely in mind. But I am confident that none of us do, for we are not God. As the apostle Paul teaches us, in this life "we see in a mirror, dimly" and not yet "face to face."

Is this too skeptical, too relativistic? I hope not! In another of his writings, Paul observes that "we have this treasure in clay jars [earthen vessels], so that it may be made clear that this extraordinary power belongs to God and does not come from us." That is a reminder of our limitations, to be sure. We are "clay jars." But God has also given us *treasure* in those clay jars! What is that treasure? He puts it this way: "[I]t is the God who said, 'Let light shine out of darkness,' who has shone in our hearts to give the light of the knowledge of the glory of God in the face of Jesus Christ." The treasure has come through our encounter with Jesus Christ, the man who was truly human—who was *in every sense* human— but through whom we most truly see God *as God truly is*.

Who is this Jesus Christ? The discovery of Christ—and of God through Christ—is no mere literary project. Preaching that is exegetically pedantic misses the point. If Christ is not in a deeper sense a living reality to us, what importance could Christ possibly have? Surely this means that what we bring out of our own experience to our interpretation of the Christ we meet in the Bible is very important. Surely the experience of others should also matter to us, of those whose first witness is recorded in scripture and also those of subsequent generations whose experience has conveyed deep truth. Surely the work of our minds in sorting it all out and applying our insights to the ongoing stream of experience and problems is also helpful. So we have a kind of fourfold approach to theological knowledge, based upon scripture, tradition, experience, and reason. This quadrilateral of sources of theological thought, though formulated specifically by United Methodists, is really implied by the work of many thinkers of other Christian traditions. To think theologically is to take each of those sources seriously, but there is no formula available to tell us exactly how.

I do want to make one point about the use of the Bible that is especially relevant to preaching. Preaching can be thoroughly, deeply "biblical" even without explicit reference to any particular biblical passage. I am not advocating the avoidance of explicit references, for on the whole it is a mistake not to include specific references. But remember it is God's word we are called to proclaim, and that word can be delivered without using the actual words of the Bible—and still be very biblical.

Why is it important to make this point? In order to see more clearly the other side of the same coin: It is possible to use the actual words of the Bible and be very *un*biblical! Specific passages can be quoted—and have been—to justify everything from genocide to polygamy, slavery, racism, the denigration of women, self-hatred, self-centeredness, and religious persecution. Therefore, to be a truly biblical preacher one must frankly accept the task of being an interpreter, struggling to understand and to help other people understand what in this vast treasure-house is the real treasure. In our use of particular biblical passages, we illuminate a deeper truth. The words always point beyond themselves; still, the words help greatly as we seek to find the treasure.

And what is that treasure? We have spoken of Christ as the true

Word of God. Who is Christ to us? How does Christ confront us in our humanity so we see through him the truth about God for us?

Perhaps the heart of it is that through Christ we confront the fact that we really do matter to God. Christ died for us while we were yet sinners. That proves God's love for us. It demonstrates God's love if we believe that Christ was fully an expression of that love. To know that we are truly beloved of God—to know that the God of all the ages cares about each one of us individually and particularly—*changes everything*. The universe of space and the eternity of time are no longer a desert—a place of desertion. We are not adrift on a sea that will ultimately swallow us up. Even in the face of all that modern people know about the universe, we *belong*. That is now our identity. So we are called to *respond* to that reality.

I shall say more about this in subsequent chapters, but this sense of belonging to God surely challenges every lesser view of our humanity at the root. It is therefore the ground out of which the prophetic word must be spoken. It is profoundly theological. No merely ideological message can convey that in our humanity we are who we are as seen in Christ. It is about justice, but not an abstract, external justice—indeed, it helps us define what justice is finally all about. It is about obligation, but it is an obligation different from the requirements of external law. It is the "obligation" to accept as a gift what God has freely given and, in our actions, to embody and truly receive the gift.

It may help, in drawing this together, to note again that the prophetic is not necessarily the controversial. Speaking to people about the great value of their lives can be a prophetic challenge to their hopelessness, but it is hardly an angry or adversarial word. When, in the Sermon on the Mount, Jesus refers to the poor peasants gathered before him as the "salt of the earth," this probably came to them as new information. When we preach to the disinherited of the earth that they, too, matter to God, this can seem flatly unbelievable (so much so that we have to do more than talk to make it seem a truth on the basis of which one could actually live). It may be an equally important word to preach to the oppressors or the self-centered, to help them see that they too are acting out a hopeless conception of themselves.

In one of our midweek communion/healing services, a homeless man came forward asking me to pray for him. He wanted to change; he didn't know how. I don't remember his exact words, nor do I remember the words of my prayer with him. I do remember taking him by the shoulder and, with a power that could only have come from God, saying to him that his life really mattered, that God really loved him, that we were there to help as a community of faith and love. And I remember how it took hold of him, that power of God's grace. And then to see him—and others like him, for he was not alone in this—in the greater congregation on a Sunday morning and to know that the proclamation of the word must be wholly consistent with that more personal moment of prayer. And to know that the reality of the church must also be consistent with that proclamation, or it will all fall apart. And to know that the realities of the more personal moment, of the congregation at worship, and of the church's own life must be able to help reconstruct one's existence in the world outside the church: That is the prophetic word as preached and enacted.

three

The Pastoral and the Prophetic

In chapter 2 we explored the deeper implications of a cardinal principle of speech: In order to communicate effectively with an audience, a pastor must share some values with the congregation. There is another, equally important principle: People are much more likely to change if they believe that the one seeking to change them really cares about them. An audience can usually sense a speaker's hostility, and that hostility can get in the way. Conversely, a speaker's positive attitude toward the audience can enhance the acceptability of unpopular ideas and appeals. I once attended a statewide candidates' training session conducted by a major political party. One of the trainers made an interesting point. He advised the candidates to conduct their campaign in such a way that undecided voters, weighing the candidates in the privacy of the voting booth, would say, "At least so-and-so is a *nice person.*" The principle I have in mind is something like that; the audience needs to feel positively related to the speaker.

Before developing the implications of this further, I want to acknowledge that sometimes the process seems to work better the other way around. The shock effect of unpleasant truth, delivered in an unpleasant way by an unpleasant person, can also be motivating. I don't know whether Jonathan Edwards was smiling at his congregation in Northampton when he delivered his classic sermon "Sinners in the Hands of an Angry God," but the words themselves were altogether negative. Referring to his listeners as "loathesome insects," he evidently scared the hell out of them. Maybe Amos was effective in that way. Fear, certainly, can be a powerful force for personal change. In the end, though, I wonder how deep the change runs if the motivation is, figuratively, that of saving one's own skin. The problem with fear as the primary basis for change is that once the fear is removed so is the motivation. Of course, that does not refer to the kind of fear that is an expression of love. One can convey that one loves another so much that one is simply driven to express fear (and try to arouse fear) about the consequences of present sins and injustices. But the main point is still love, and it makes a huge difference when the preacher is known to care about the people of the congregation.

So what are we to make of this principle as it applies to prophetic preaching? Does it not mean that the prophetic message will be better heard if the preacher is also a good pastor? Members of a congregation may still reject the message—especially if it is not well thought out. But they will not reject it because they have previously rejected the messenger! I don't want to make this seem too simple. In chapter 10 I will take up the question of criticism, noting that a seriously prophetic message will often lead to opposition no matter how good a pastor the preacher is. But the situation will always be improved if the preacher is a good pastor.

Stories abound on this subject. One of my favorites concerns Ernest Fremont Tittle, one of the greatest preachers of the mid-twentieth century. He held a number of fairly radical (and arguably prophetic) views that were not broadly shared by his congregation at First Methodist Church, Evanston, Illinois. It is said that at one point a serious move was mounted to have him dismissed from the pulpit. But, at a key meeting, one of the leading laymen—widely known for his conservatism—put a stop to the idea with a moving speech about how Dr. Tittle had stayed up all night with the layman's dying wife.

If caring for the congregation is a good principle for effective prophetic preaching, I am not sure it is one that can be followed for that reason alone. In other words, I do not believe one can fake it. A pastor cannot just pretend to love the congregation so the congregation will accept what is being said. It is necessary *actually* to love the congregation, even the most recalcitrant sinners among them. Surely this at least means that spiritual preparation to preach is quite as important as the crafting of sermons, and that spiritual preparation is growth in love. Surely it also means reaching out to serve even when one does not much feel like it.

Pastoral service is not always pleasant. Sometimes we are just not in the mood. I well remember one Saturday night when, in the small hours, I was rudely awakened by the telephone. It was the emergency room at George Washington University Hospital, five or six miles from our home. The caller was a nurse there. Somebody, not of my own church, had just died. The family was gathered and wanted a United Methodist pastor to come pray with them. I was the only one the nurse had succeeded in reaching, and would I come? But this is *Saturday night,* I thought. I don't know them; they're not members of my church; this is going to ruin me for tomorrow morning. I didn't voice those thoughts. I said, a little gruffly, "Yes, I'll come." Driving along in that frame of mind, it's a wonder I didn't have an accident getting there. I was still half asleep, but also angry at having been disturbed. On arrival, I was greeted by the grieving family. They were obviously very religious people. They were hurt beyond words by their loss, and they were reaching out for "some word of the Lord." All of my self-absorbed anger fell away. I was exactly where I needed to be in that moment, and I knew it. After spending time with the family, I returned home—not so much drained as deepened, maybe even refreshed in spirit. My sermon the next day did not suffer; even if it had, it would have been worth it. In the long run, such pastoral experiences contribute greatly to our preaching.

Let me state the principle in an academic way. A C-plus sermon will be perceived as B-plus or A-minus if the preacher is viewed as a friend; an A-plus sermon will be demoted to a B or lower if the preacher comes across as uncaring.

But this is not finally an academic principle, not finally even a question of effectiveness. It has the closest possible relationship to the content, not just the form, of preaching. If the whole point of the prophetic word is God's love, how on earth can that message be heard if it is not expressed in a context of love? If the very concept of justice finally depends, for its ultimate meaning, upon the love of God, how can even that word take on reality apart from love? We cannot preach about love unlovingly; it is a self-contradiction. The great nineteenth-century preacher Phillips Brooks used to define preaching as "truth through personality." I could quarrel with the adequacy of that definition, but wasn't he on the right track? The very being of the preacher must be consistent with the spoken words, lest the effect of the words be dissipated. Worse, a gross inconsistency between the message and the messenger will *destroy* the message. It will be a visible demonstration of its powerlessness. If even the messenger, the preacher, doesn't believe in it enough to live it out, why should anybody else?

I realize those are frightening words. Are we not called to preach even though we are still sinners? That, too, we must acknowledge and take into account. To be a pastor is to be in touch with one's humanity and to acknowledge one's limitations. In the end, it does not damage the prophetic message for prophets to speak of a truth and love by which they too are challenged. We cannot preach of the sins and injustices of others without being even more conscious of how far we ourselves have fallen short.

Being a pastor contributes to the effectiveness of prophetic preaching in another way: Good pastors simply *know* more about the human conditions of which they speak. In the course of the 1960 presidential campaign, John F. Kennedy gave a major speech on poverty. An opposition newspaper attacked the speech in a front-page editorial. What, the editorial inquired, is all this business about poverty? The writer was sure it was all overblown, since he himself didn't personally know even one poor person! I'm sure there must have been hundreds of pastors in the city who could have improved the writer's case information—probably with many thousands of actual examples. Having experienced human problems directly and personally confers enormous moral authority as one ventures to speak about them. It is a natural temptation to give too great weight to emotional anecdotes, and I am not suggesting that. Individual cases must be related responsibly to the wider picture. But when they are, the effect can be awesome. Even when a pastor does not choose to use those experiences specifically, having had them greatly enhances his or her self-confidence in voicing the message.

Being a good pastor also makes it much easier to know the mental state of those to whom one is speaking—their values, their uncertainties, the life experiences through which they will refract whatever they hear, their prejudices, their nobler instincts. It makes it easier to avoid the shut-off valves in their minds—the things that will stop them from doing any further thinking. It will help one know better the caveats or qualifications one had better introduce into one's sermons, so the listeners won't constantly be saying to themselves, "Yes, but."

As a theology professor, most of my preaching for many years was to congregations for which I had no pastoral role or responsibility. Even in such settings I was usually able to get through on the basis of other kinds of pastoral experience. But I did not really know the people with whom I was speaking. I recognized this all the more clearly when I moved directly into a position of pastoral responsibility, preaching to people I came to know and love as individuals. I realize what a difference it makes to be able to look out at a congregation on Sunday morning, recognize people, and remember what they have been through and what they face. Here is a family that has suffered tragedy through alcoholism. That fact will affect how I speak of problems of addiction. Here is someone who has been unemployed for some time. That will affect my dealing with economic questions. Here are people who have wanted very deeply to have children but could not. That cannot help but influence anything I say about the joys and responsibilities of parenting. Here are parents having great difficulty with teenage children or couples in troubled marriages—facts I must remember as I preach about family values. It is not that the presence of people undergoing difficulty should lead us to avoid anything related to their problems. Quite the contrary: It should lead us to help them see those problems in the light of the gospel of God's love. Knowing people well can help us find the right words.

On a recent Sunday our church was picketed by an extremist group with a mean-spirited anti-gay agenda. They were surly in appearance; their signs were hateful. My inclination is to ignore this kind of action, trusting that the congregation will be able to put it in better perspective if the pastor treats it as a nonevent, so during the first service I said nothing. But afterward a gay member of our congregation, visibly shaken by the hate group, asked if there was something I could say. I pondered the question as the second service began, looking out at the congregation and seeing a number of others for whom the picketing might also have been a traumatic experience. In my sermon for that day, "Unless the Lord Guards the City," I had a section on the church as a zone of security in the midst of the troubled world, a natural point to speak of the hate outside and the love inside and how everybody needs to feel they are accepted unreservedly in the community of faith. The inclusion of a few words of this kind obviously helped the congregation, but I would not have done it without the pastoral relationships.

The Community of Faith

I have written, thus far, of the pastoral context as though it were simply the relationship of a pastor to the people whom he or she is called to serve. That relationship is very real and very important. But a pastoral relationship must not be seen as exclusively one-on-one. It is a quality of community life. Indeed, no pastor can possibly keep up alone with the personal needs of a whole congregation, unless the group is *very* small. Even then, the reality of Christian love is undermined if the love is not in some sense communal, people in the congregation caring about one another, a caring that spills over into the world beyond the church. A caring congregation is a marvelous seedbed for genuinely prophetic preaching. The congregation is already experiencing together what the message is finally all about. There remains room for disagreement, of course. But it is disagreement in a form that leads to mutual growth, not to mutual destructiveness.

Is this sense of community possible in every congregation? I am convinced that it is, even in an urban setting where people travel considerable distances to get to church and where many of the members do not interact in the same places of business or residential neighborhoods. I do not want to idealize the church I know best, for it has not succeeded in drawing everybody into a circle of mutual caring. And yet it has managed to overcome some of the obstacles of distance and diversity—perhaps turning them from obstacles into assets. Our youth group, for instance, has scarcely more than two young people who attend the same high school. Moreover, because of the distances many travel, they are not able to meet on Sunday evenings. And yet they have developed a remarkably close fellowship, with periodic weekend retreats and service projects that are bonding experiences even as they are works of charity. The congregation itself has a variety of ways of expressing its commonality. One of the most interesting is the recruitment each Sunday of volunteers to contact those who are in hospitals, or who are grieving the loss of loved ones, or who have experienced some unusually joyful event, such as a wedding or a birth. The recruitment occurs in the worship service itself. The subliminal message is, This could be you in this situation, and we would all care in the same way if it were. Even visitors are made to feel that, at least for this Sunday, this is also *their* church.

Again, I do not want to paint too rosy a picture. There must be many churches that do much better, each in its own way. But think of such churches as at least pointing in the right direction and reminding us that the pastoral reality is that of a whole community; it is not limited to the relationship between the professional clergyperson and the parishioners.

While the reality is much more comprehensive, the preacher can do much to reinforce it. One way is in our sermons. Sermons help to define the social reality of the church as a reflection of the deeper theological reality. We all need to be reminded, constantly, that our mutual caring within the community of faith is a visible sign to the world of what God's purposes are for the whole human family. And thus our mutual caring extends into the community beyond the church and is warmly hospitable to those who enter.

Pastoral Trust

I wish to make another point concerning the relationship between a pastor and members of the congregation. A congregation must be able to trust its pastor and preacher not to abuse the enormous privileges of the office. For instance, one does not divulge confidences shared in a pastoral setting. Sometimes a sermon illustration derived from pastoral experience can provide exactly the right homiletical note. But it should be used only with uncoerced permission. In my experience, permission is often readily given, but one must never presume upon that. Even if such permission can be gotten, illustrations should not be used when the story or quotation might reflect badly upon a person who is readily identifiable. When pastoral illustrations are used, it is also a good idea to note clearly that it is with permission. Otherwise, some people in the congregation might be leery of bringing confidences to the pastor in future, lest they appear in sermon form. A number of denominations, my own included, specify in church law that pastoral confidences may not be divulged. Apart from instances where a pastor must report or intervene for the sake of the life and health of third parties (such as abused children), that rule should be observed scrupulously.

Obviously, a pastor must also be absolutely trustworthy in not exploiting the prestige and charisma that often, like it or not, are conferred with the position. There have been far too many illustrations of such exploitation in recent years, instances of preachers with enormous gifts using them to exploit vulnerable people. The result of such indiscretion is always at least a four-way tragedy. First, there is the injury done to the vulnerable parishioner. Second, there is the damage done to the pastor, whose loss of integrity has diminished his or her personal fulfillment in ministry. Third, there is damage to this and other congregations in the weakening of confidence in *other* pastors. Fourth, there will be people who lose faith in the message itself. Often enough, the message has been much truer than the flawed messenger—but the damage has nevertheless been done. The temptations are often proportional to a preacher's gifts. The more attractive and winsome the preacher, the greater the positive response. It is all too easy for gifted preachers to take everything personally—that is, to accept adulation as their personal due. Placed on a pedestal, preachers can come to think of themselves as being above ordinary standards of behavior. Martin Luther's famous sacristy prayer, to be prayed before preaching, includes the earnest plea that, after preaching the word of God, the preacher should then seek diligently to perform it—with all the glory going to God.

The Pastoral Leads to the Prophetic

Sometimes it is said that the pastoral is in conflict with the prophetic. This simply is not so. The prophetic is greatly enhanced by the pastoral. And by the same token, the pastoral is enhanced by the prophetic. If by prophetic we mean our reach for the deep truth about God's love as it is expressed in the circumstances of human life, then it is not possible to minister to the real needs of people without being prophetic. Sometimes, as we have seen, that means a message about the true identity of people, from which they have allowed themselves to be distracted. To be a faithful pastor is to call people back to who they really are and help them organize their lives in accordance with those deeper insights of faith. It is also to draw people into more faithful expressions of life in their world of institutions and power.

A person of faith may, as an individual, express caring love for those nearest at hand. But if, at the same time, that person is deeply involved in institutions that are in contradiction to faithful love, he or she suffers an objective loss of centered selfhood.

Two of the great Christian prophets of the twentieth century saw this point clearly. Walter Rauschenbusch, the foremost theologian of the early twentieth-century social gospel movement, provided a classic definition of a Christian social order by observing that in it bad people are forced to do good things. An unchristian social order, on the other hand, is one in which good people are forced to do bad things! There may be an element of Christian triumphalism in the way he expressed his point, but is that not a penetrating insight into how the structures of power in which we live point us either toward good or toward evil? And if we are working for institutions that are contributing to injustice, our lives are in self-contradiction. We cannot easily escape the dilemma, for no institutions are perfectly pure. But a pastoral relationship can hardly overlook the problem. To be pastoral is to help people work through the dilemmas of living in unjust settings. To be pastoral is also to be prophetic.

The other twentieth-century prophet was Reinhold Niebuhr, who reminded us in his 1932 book *Moral Man and Immoral Society* that one can be quite moral as an individual but at the same time be a participant in vast immoralities at the social level. Later, as Niebuhr observed the effects of good laws in curbing the worst immoralities of individual racism, he remarked that sometimes the terms should be reversed to read "immoral man and moral society." But the point remains either way: To minister to people in a pastoral way, we cannot avoid their broader social relationships.

It is not always easy to correlate the pastoral with the prophetic. At least superficially, the two can impose different kinds of demands. In the end, though, they are two sides of the same coin. One cannot be very prophetic without being pastoral; one cannot be very pastoral without being prophetic.

four

The Liturgical Setting

Taken as a part of the liturgy, the sermon is the point where the worship experience as a whole can be drawn together. Good preaching appeals to the heart as well as the mind. But the sermon, relative to other aspects of liturgy, may proportionately be more addressed to the mind. It helps us see the wholeness of the faith in its implications for all aspects of our life. It is easy and natural for the sermon to draw attention to other parts of the liturgy, helping a congregation to see the prayers and hymns and scripture readings in a fresh light. Good preaching will enhance the impact of other aspects of the liturgy, just as they will enhance the sermon.

There was a time, happily now past, when worship was understood in many Protestant churches only to be a preliminary to the main event, the Sunday sermon. Worship was designed to set the stage, to create an emotional climate of receptivity. No one was expected to take the content of worship too seriously, if it was noticed at all. A certain approach to prophetic preaching could, and sometimes did, reinforce this condescending attitude toward worship: If social justice is what really matters, then worship can be viewed as a distraction—or even a subversion of the main point.

"I hate, I despise your festivals," exclaimed Amos, "and I take no delight in your solemn assemblies." Yet does not even that sharp-tongued rebuke of Israelite worship make the point that worship is very important in respect to prophetic ministry? Worship is not a neutral filler in the life of the assembled congregation. It is loaded with value assumptions, often implicit, sometimes clearly evident. Amos was judging worship that substituted aesthetic values for the central value of God's justice as it must be enacted in human relationships. "Take away from me the noise of your songs; I will not listen to the melody of your harps. But let justice roll down like waters, and righteousness like an ever-flowing stream" (Amos 5:21, 23–24). One wonders how Amos might have responded to social justice set to music or, superb rhetorician that he was, to litanies and prayers that draw the worshiper deeply and sensitively into the meaning of the world's brokenness. How might he have felt about some of the social gospel hymns: "Where Cross the Crowded Ways of Life" or "In Christ There Is No East or West" or the earlier "Once to Every Man and Nation"?

Worship, on the face of it, is loaded with themes that reflect or express values. Prayers, hymns, creeds, responses all evoke in people understandings of God and of God's purposes. All are profoundly suggestive of what our personal and communal life is meant to be.

The sermon does not exist in isolation from those elements of worship. Rather, it is a part of worship. A sermon, a prayer, a hymn can be preached, prayed, or sung all by itself. But when it is, we have a sense of incompleteness. That is particularly so of the sermon. For a sermon, all by itself, is one-way communication without specific opportunity for congregational participation. That is even true in those ecclesial traditions in which congregations are expected to respond to telling phrases with an "amen" or a "preach."

A subtle point lurks here. When the focus is entirely upon the sermon, it is all the more difficult for even the sermon to focus upon God. Worship draws us into something much larger than ourselves, reinforcing how the sermon must point beyond itself. When everything centers on the sermon, members of a worshiping congregation may feel this is quite "normal"—while at the same time many will feel a certain incompleteness. Something is missing.

Preachers themselves can reflect on the dryness of seeking to preach in a nonworshiping setting. Consider, for example, the artificiality most preachers have experienced in their practice sermons in seminary. Preaching to fellow students and to an evaluating professor is bad enough. Doing it in a completely nonliturgical setting makes it all the more artificial. My personal experience of this was quite traumatic. The only time I ever had a complete memory lapse—total wipeout—was in my own seminary homiletics class, preaching a practice sermon. Fortunately for me, the professor responded with kindness. I have never forgotten the lesson. Now, as an occasional teacher of such classes, I invite seminarians to select a hymn to be sung before their practice sermon. That helps, although it is certainly minimal. It does reinforce the great importance of the liturgy and of preaching as an aspect—not the whole—of liturgy. Moreover, the worship setting makes preaching so much easier for the preacher. The climate of shared values, whose importance we noted in chapter 2, is set. The congregation is likely to be much more attentive and receptive. And the preacher is less likely to be self-conscious.

How Worship
Reinforces the Message

It is a mistake, it seems to me, to try to have every aspect of the liturgy conform precisely to the theme of the sermon. Worship speaks to us in a variety of ways and bespeaks the transcendence of God. But things can also be incorporated into worship that are in direct conflict with the prophetic message. Hate, prejudice, self-righteousness, materialism—almost any imaginable non-Christian attitude can be expressed in the materials of a worship service.

As an illustration of self-righteousness, I recall the prayer for enemies in the otherwise acceptable hymnal used by chaplains in the U.S. armed forces. In that Cold War–era prayer, the sins of the enemies, including their designs to enslave us, are paraded at some length. Only toward the end is there an acknowledgment that we who pray may bear some responsibility for the enmity! That prayer, because it is so extreme, illustrates the importance of how we pray for others.

A prayer can be the vehicle of either compassion or self-righteousness; sometimes it can be self-righteousness masked as compassion. A group of Methodist missionaries in a Central American language school were outnumbered in the school by missionaries of fundamentalist churches, who dominated the daily worship services in the school chapel. Bemoaning the judgmentalism to which she and her fellow Methodists were regularly subjected in these services, one older missionary student exclaimed, "we're being prayed for—*viciously!*" Perhaps the prayers were not intended to be adversarial. But when other categories of people are singled out in prayers petitioning God to change them, the note of self-righteousness is not far behind. Jesus' caustic parable about the Pharisee and the tax collector (Luke 18:9–14) makes this point. The self-righteous Pharisee thanks God that he is "not like other people: thieves, rogues, adulterers, or even like this tax collector." The tax collector, all too aware of his sins, prays simply, "God, be merciful to me, a sinner." And Jesus is clear that it is the tax collector, not the Pharisee, whose prayer is acceptable to God.

If such prayers can be in direct conflict with a prophetic message, they also can and should reinforce it. A prayer addressed to God reinforces our sense of awe and wonder in the presence of the One who transcends our smallness of mind and spirit. Prayer can naturally and easily encourage the attitude of humility, helping us to avoid the temptations of self-righteousness. Real prayer does not instruct God so much as it brings our concerns to God and opens us up to a new way of seeing things. Prayer reinforces our trust in the love of God, and, filled with the love of God, we are drawn closer to those from whom we have been estranged. A real "prayer for enemies," for instance, will remind us that there is no human enemy who is not also loved by God.

The Subtleties of
Thanksgiving and Confession

Prayers of thanksgiving frequently reflect our own values. What, indeed, do we say we are thankful for? What hand has God played in our receiving what we take to be gifts? For instance, in prayer we may voice our gratitude to God that we were born in such a wonderful country, blessed with freedom, and so on. What are the implied judgments here about other countries? What is the implied conception of freedom? In context, does it seem to include freedom of the "God helps those who help themselves and the devil takes the hindmost" variety? Or when we give thanks for our material blessings, does the prayer imply that we (in contrast with some other people) *deserve* what we have gotten? Or that God has chosen to bless us, and not them, materially? We thank God for employment, or success in a competition, or even the blessings of health. What are the unemployed, the losers, the diseased and handicapped supposed to pray? Something like "Thanks a lot, God"? Prayer that is cleansed of self-righteousness and competitiveness can still voice our deep gratitude for the gift of life, the capacity to love, and the opportunity to serve.

What is true of prayers of thanksgiving is also true of confession. What we confess reflects what we value. For instance, confession can be framed provisionally to read, "*If* I have sinned against anybody, Lord, please forgive me." The impression here is that I probably have not sinned against anybody, at least not very seriously, but, just in case, I trust you will forgive me for it. Even when a prayer is framed specifically, the sins we actually confess may be comparatively trivial, while the sins that remain unacknowledged—and therefore unconfessed—may be the truly serious ones. God may smile, figuratively speaking, over the little immaturities and be deeply grieved over the broken relationships we have caused and the massive injustices we have tolerated. An image from the television film series *Holocaust* comes to mind. An officer in the German military, home from duty in one of the extermination camps for Christmas holiday, joyfully sings Christmas carols as his family gathers around the piano. Such things actually did happen and do happen. In her report on the Eichmann trial, Barbara Tuchman notes that Adolf Eichmann—who contributed to the deaths of more than a million Jews in the Holocaust—when examined psychologically expressed remorse only at his disobedience to some of the bureaucratic orders. What we confess is an important indicator of what we consider important.

It is usually a mistake to frame corporate prayers of confession, which people are more or less required to recite, around sins that people do not believe they have committed or do not consider to be sins at all. But prayer can still help open us up to the consequences of our attitudes and actions. For example, a prayer of confession for helping to support capital punishment would not be convincing to people who believe in the appropriateness of capital punishment. But a prayer for a condemned person and his or her family that touched upon their humanity and the tragedy of what had brought them to this point could be accompanied by confession that as a community we have not been as sensitive to that human reality as God is. And such a prayer should speak similarly about the victims of the condemned person's crime.

Worship and Community

The liturgy also symbolizes our sense of the meaning and limits of community. A highly nationalistic liturgy virtually identifies the nation with God's intended kingdom. A highly individualized form of spirituality lacks even that degree of communal awareness. But the liturgy can draw people into a universal sense of God's family. Our prayers reach out to the suffering of people in faraway lands. Our hymns celebrate the oneness of all humanity. Even the nonhuman aspects of creation can be seen as a part of God's wider community. Through hymn and prayer, those who have been stigmatized and ostracized from community can be explicitly and lovingly included.

In recent years, theologians like Rosemary Radford Ruether and hymn writers like Brian Wren have helped us see that the language of liturgy itself conveys a value message that is either more or less inclusive. The church at large has not yet quite digested the importance of this, but the words we use in addressing God sometimes contain important implications about human relationships. If God is always identified in male-specific language (Father, King, etc.), that may not be intended to exclude women (for the Father also loves women, of course, and to be a beloved daughter is hardly to be excluded). Nevertheless, such terminology for God, if always used, does convey that God somehow is more *like* men. And if men are more Godlike than women, has not a higher value been placed upon them?

How Preaching Helps
Focus Worship

So what are the implications of these points for prophetic preaching? Clearly we must pay attention to the liturgy lest it undercut the message of the sermon. But more than that, the sermon is opportunity for explanation and qualification and application. The importance of that was brought home to me a few years ago when I was preaching on a text from Leviticus that had been read earlier in the service as the Old Testament lesson. The passage included one of the ritual-law prohibitions involving women having a menstrual flow, the effect of which, to modern ears, is distinctly critical toward and negative about women. That part of the passage was not involved in any way in the sermon, and I had just ignored it. A day or so later I received a highly aggrieved letter from a woman in the congregation. She believed, and rightly so, that whenever such readings appear in the service without explanation or interpretation they carry the implication of corporate believing—that it is normal, in this congregation, for us all to believe this thing that has just been read to us as sacred scripture. She thought I should have made a distancing comment about that part of the reading, either at the time it was read or when Leviticus was referred to in the sermon, and she was exactly right.

The same point should apply to any other aspect of the traditional liturgy that now runs counter to a deeper level of moral sensibility. As noted in the last section, much liturgical language continues to invoke the divine name in predominantly male imagery, conveying the notion that God is more male than female and implying that men are more like God than women are. What could be a profounder basis for real inequality between the genders than that—especially when complemented by scriptural passages specifically relegating women to lesser roles in church and society? Surely it is a proper task for preaching to explain the deeper truth and to help a congregation understand the cultural background out of which such language has come down to us. People find liberation in such sermonic explanations.

I am among those who do not wish to rewrite the scriptures or to abandon aspects of Christian tradition that are no longer compatible with moral sensibilities. When we do this it is too easy to throw the baby out with the bathwater. The Leviticus in which narrow cultic purity laws are to be found is the same Leviticus in which we encounter great concern for strangers and sojourners and poor people within the community. The Augustine who had narrow attitudes on some subjects was the same theologian whose deep understanding of God's grace and of the meaning of human community continues to enlighten Christian thought.

But if we avail ourselves of the treasures of scripture and tradition, as we should, we must also explain them with greater care and ensure that the blind spots of an earlier age not be perpetuated along with the treasures. The sermon can be especially helpful at exactly that point as it invites a congregation to think more clearly and to feel more deeply.

five

From Generalities
to Specifics

A few years ago, after preaching a sermon on peace (text: Isaiah 32:16–18), I received a letter questioning whether I had gotten too specific.

> Regarding the sermon last Sunday: I for one felt that there were several "Presidential policy options" embedded in the latter part of your remarks, and I think it is preferable to avoid such specific recommendations when you have "the most prominent parishioner" caught in the congregation. The earlier part of the sermon, when dealing with the exegesis of Isaiah and the theology of Barth, was interesting and sufficiently remote from the current choices facing the country.

My attention was, of course, riveted by the last line, with its implication that preaching should remain "remote from the current choices facing the country."

In fairness to the writer, we should remember that similar views have been held by substantial numbers of preachers—and professors of homiletics, for that matter. The letter writer was not necessarily saying that the gospel should not be applied to specific situations. It is possible that the question was rather who should apply it, and when, and under what circumstances. Perhaps the writer only meant that you shouldn't preach on national issues and options when the President is in attendance—although the implication of that might be that one should avoid dealing with the choices *anybody* present in the congregation might be facing. Possibly the writer thought that the specific implications of the message should be left to the listener to determine and that it would be both undesirable and unnecessary for the preacher to draw them out.

Some Preliminary Thoughts

A case can be made for such a perspective, particularly if the message is thoroughly biblical. The message of the text can be illustrated, and even applied, in a general way. But to apply it specifically can—it is alleged—rob it of the text's inherent force. To go the further step of applying it specifically to an actual situation might put some people on the defensive, making it more difficult for the gospel to penetrate the defenses people put up when they are under psychological attack. If that line of reasoning seems too cowardly, there is the further argument that some of the people in the pews may know more about how the message should be applied in their own lives than any preacher possibly could. For instance, a sermon on God's special concern for the poor needs to be applied to modern business and economics. But what preacher could possibly know more about the application than the businesspeople and economists out there in the pews? Better (the argument might go) for the preacher to draw people into the deep message of the Bible. Once captivated by the message, they will feel driven to modify their own lives by that gospel, and they will know better how this is to be done. So a case can be made.

But there is more to be said. In a thoughtful commentary on biblical preaching, David Buttrick questions even the basic assumption about biblical preaching. Criticizing Karl Barth, the Swiss theologian who so greatly influenced twentieth-century biblical preaching, Buttrick asserts:

> In the thought of Karl Barth, the Bible alone was the source of revelation; there was no other knowledge of God, no natural theology, no insights, no wisdoms, no truth to be gleaned from the human world. In a way, the world was regarded as an adversary. Therefore, preachers were *not* called to relate to the world, but simply to expound biblical truth to the faithful in church.[3]

While acknowledging the importance of scripture in preaching, Buttrick asks whether Protestants can "begin to admit that the Bible is, in and of itself, insufficient?"[4] It is not a book of magic. It has to be interpreted, and everything depends on *how* it is interpreted. The gospel, which is bigger than the Bible, draws us toward the world's hurts:

> The church is primarily a witness in the world; we tell good news of God. But we cannot ignore the contexts in which our speaking occurs. If we preach to persons who are victims of grinding poverty with no concern for social solutions to their poverty, as if saving souls had nothing to do with food on the table, we will misrepresent Jesus Christ. . . . [T]he gospel may well call me personally to believe and repent. But surely the gospel may also call General Motors to repentance or, yes, the Pentagon and the United States of America. People now feel trapped in systems that are both huge and sinful. We have begun to realize that sin is a captivity; we sinners live in bondage.[5]

Buttrick's larger point is that drawing people into the world of the Bible without thoughtful grappling with the problems of the age does a disservice to the gospel, no matter how faithful a particular sermon may be to a particular text.

Of course, the same point can be made about preaching that ignores the Bible. Topical sermons can be constructed around broad themes (or no discernible theme at all), illustrated with touching stories of human interest, and enlivened with a few jokes, all the while avoiding any application to the real world of hurt and injustice. Such preaching is not without precedent! But what is the point? Preaching that is inapplicable to the actual lives of real people, living in a real world, is of little use.

Is it true that the congregation can best be trusted to make the specific and appropriate connections? Sometimes it does work that way. A biblical passage or theological truth, artfully illustrated (though without being pointed at a particular contemporary target), can indeed draw people into an application of the truth to their own lives. Sometimes, indeed, that is the most effective homiletical strategy. I recall preaching once on a more general theme related to grace and forgiveness. I wanted to apply this to the issue of capital punishment, but I did not wish in this sermon to provide a rounded treatment of the death penalty. Instead, I recounted the response of a murder victim's brother to the impending execution of his sister's murderer. There was no question of the condemned man's guilt—he had long since acknowledged and repented the deed. His appeals had run out, and now it was only a question whether the state governor would commute his sentence to life imprisonment or allow the execution to proceed. The brother appealed to the governor to spare the man's life, saying he was sure his sister would not have wanted the man's death. The appeal was phrased with eloquent grace. Recounting the story in my sermon, I then said I did not know whether I would have had the grace to respond in this way had it been my loved one, but I was sure that what that brother had to say "came straight from the heart of God." This was not a complete treatment of the capital punishment issue; obviously, much more needs to be said. And yet I suspect most of the members of the gathered congregation got the point without the need for further elaboration.

Some Specificity Is Important

On occasion, maybe even frequently, a general theme sermon is the best strategy for getting at deeper moral issues and having them resonate with a congregation. But can we rely upon that alone? I do not think so—for four reasons.

In the first place, if we are relying upon emotional stories without drawing out their implications rationally, the effect may be only emotional and short-lived. People may also be led to treat the particular illustration as an exception, so that a preacher's words have almost no impact and leave the listener's overall view more or less intact. Yes, this murder victim's brother was filled with God's grace; maybe I should also aspire to such heights of forgiving love. Yes, this particular repentant criminal is worthy of consideration, perhaps even a commuted sentence. But on the whole, we need capital punishment to deter crime and vindicate justice against outrageous behavior and bring closure to surviving loved ones who are not as saintly as the brother in the story. Such thoughts can lead a listener to conclude that it is possible to feel good about the noble spirituality that has just been portrayed in story form without changing one's opinions in the slightest. The story may have made a contribution, but to be effective in the long run it may require more specificity of application.

Second, when we are not specific enough we can easily leave the impression that specifics aren't important—that only broad general principles matter. But the devil is (truly) in the details! If we are dealing with sin, either personal or social, it is important sufficiently to name the evil to be sure it is understood for what it is. After all, it is not evil in general or sin in general that obscures the glory of God in our lives. Rather, it is evil and sin expressed in very particular ways that need to be diagnosed and treated. Equally so, there are angels lurking in the details. It is not goodness in general or love in general but goodness and love also expressed in quite particular ways that need to be pursued. It is not possible to pursue either sin or love into all the hidden places. But if the gospel is to be proclaimed rightly, it must be with sufficient specificity that there can be no mistake about it: The gospel is about *all* of life, not just some place of spiritual retreat.

Third, prophetic preaching engages the mind as well as the heart. Preachers must be prepared to say *why* something is or is not so, and it is difficult to see how we can do that without providing a bit of detail. Does this rob the listener of space in which to do this thinking personally? Not necessarily. In fact, it may challenge the listener to do more thinking, not less. Much depends, of course, on how it is done. But the prophetic tradition, from early biblical times, has seen excellent illustrations of serious rational thought alongside its poetry and passion.

Fourth, while there may well be persons in the pews who know more about a particular topic than we do, there are not likely to be people there who know *everything* that needs to be known. Even experts are constricted in their expertise to specialized areas of competence. Moreover, they are not as likely to have struggled to make the connections between their areas of expertise and the gospel. A technical expert may be a deeply committed Christian but one whose expertise is somehow insulated from the faith he or she professes. So, when the preacher ventures an application of the gospel in somebody else's field of factual expertise, it may help that person make the connections or it may force that person to struggle a bit more with a fragmented faith and a fragmented life. This can be true even when the preacher's own grasp of the connections is unsure. The mere fact that the pastor is trying to make the connections from the pulpit can lead a congregation to more serious efforts to understand how the gospel relates to life.

A Place for Topical Preaching?

Should all preaching be biblical in the classical sense of being centered on a text, the meaning and implications of which are drawn forth for the congregation?

We have noted David Buttrick's comment that the gospel is more than the Bible. Surely he is right about that, just as he rightly notes that the earliest Christians had somehow to get along without a New Testament—and with an Old Testament canon that remained somewhat uncertain. The Bible bears witness to that gospel; it is not the gospel itself.

Still, the Bible *is* the prime witness. One does not have to be a biblical literalist, accepting every part of the Bible as a direct communication from God, of equal authority, truth, and value, to acknowledge the foundational nature of scripture. It is still true that everything about the gospel can be found there, except for the specifics of contemporary application. In the classic formulation, everything needful of salvation is to be found in the Bible. That can be affirmed even when one feels compelled to say that the Bible also contains material that, if pursued mechanically, would take you *away* from the gospel.

Returning to the issue of whether all preaching should be biblical, the next question must be, Is there any place for topical preaching that takes a subject and develops it without specific dependency upon a particular passage?

One can surely say that all preaching should be theological. It

should all have something to say about why the subject matters
ultimately and thus has some connection with the gospel. Any
sermon that is in that sense theological will also be biblical. But
that does not mean it necessarily is grounded in any one particular text or passage. It is possible to preach about the witness of the
Bible, taken as a whole, in relation to a contemporary problem. I
would not do it often, but in a pastor's homiletical repertory there
may be some point in an occasional sermon that more or less sys-
tematically gets at a realm of human life or thought. What, for instance, is the significance of political life (as a whole) in relation
to the gospel? Or economic life, or sexuality, or race relations, or
international society? Such a sermon, possibly incorporated in a
sermon series, might serve as a kind of road map for a whole area
of human life, helping the listeners to think things through in relation to the faith they profess. Such road maps can help overcome
the fragmentation of so much religious life, preparing people not
only for personal decision-making and intimate relationships but
also for the broader responsibilities of citizenship.

Such occasional sermons serve yet another function: They
challenge the preacher to think things through more carefully.
Having thought things through, it is easier to deal with little bits
and pieces when one is later pursuing a different homiletical strategy.

Still, a steady diet of topical sermons can be less nurturing of
the faith. Biblical preaching that is grounded in particular passages,
exploring the nuances of meaning and applying them in a penetrating way, can be a better channel for the prophetic. The authority of the Bible, after all, is not derived from the arbitrary
decisions of the church. Ultimately, the Bible has authority because so much speaks to us so deeply that we find ourselves compelled by it. The preacher can help unlock the treasure for a
congregation.

Novelist and preacher Frederick Buechner raises serious questions about preaching that does not reach below the surface of
broad ideas. He tells of an experience teaching a seminary class
on preaching in which a number of the students were humanist
atheists. Unable to believe in God, such students thought of

preaching as speaking of *ideas* of peace, kindness, social responsibility, and the like. Buechner reports that this provided him with the realization that "if ideas were all I had to preach, I would take up some other line of work." He had come to understand in a new way that preaching

> is to proclaim a Mystery before which, before whom, even our most exalted ideas turn to straw. It is also to proclaim this Mystery with a passion that ideas alone have little to do with. It is to try to put the Gospel into words not the way you would compose an essay but the way you would write a poem or a love letter—putting your heart into it, your own excitement, most of all your own life. It is to speak words that you hope may, by grace, be bearers not simply of new understanding but of new life both for the ones you are speaking to and also for you.[6]

Buechner's perspective cuts in several directions. It certainly calls into question any sermons on ideas and issues that are more lecture than sermon. And it forces us to abandon a mechanical kind of biblical preaching. I suppose it would be possible to preach a "topical" sermon, at least one that is not tied to any specific texts, provided the theological content drew one into the deep realms of faith and mystery. Such preaching could be deeply prophetic. I find Buechner's perspective, like all his writing, very attractive. Still, I would not be so dismissive of ideas and applications. Speaking from and to the heart is important in all preaching, but the mind had better be engaged as well. Otherwise, what passes for depth and mystery can too easily dissolve into sentimentality.

Being Just Specific Enough

In chapters 8 and 9 I will consider questions of method in prophetic preaching, while noting some of the pitfalls to be avoided. But before leaving this discussion of specificity in prophetic preaching, I must add that much of what we preach depends on how and when. There needs to be enough specificity to make the point that the great truths of the gospel must be applied or they don't count. There needs to be enough to "convict" sinners of their actual sin, that is, convince them that they really are enmeshed in sin from which they need to be liberated. There needs to be enough to suggest concrete possibilities, lest we feel that the gospel is nice but not very realistic in such a world. But much truly does have to be left for the imagination. Artful preaching has enough detail to suggest to every listener that much more remains to be spelled out than the preacher can possibly do in the allotted time, and that we all have to keep working at it.

But this also suggests another point. In applying the gospel to the complexities of real life, a preacher must not claim greater expertise than he or she actually possesses. It is important to do one's homework, and even then to acknowledge that one is not infallible. It is possible to preach with conviction, even with passion, about particular problems, even while acknowledging that there is more to be known. Our prayer should always be, in effect, "O God, when I am right help me to be as grace-filled and persuasive as possible, but when I am wrong let my wrongful words be corrected as quickly by others (or at least be quickly forgotten by them)." It does not diminish the force of prophetic preaching to be open to further dialogue and criticism.

The more technically detailed one's message is, the more one is likely to need correction. But that fact should not be an inhibition. Sometimes it is better to lay out a flawed viewpoint that at least opens up a subject that is crying out for attention than to allow the subject to remain hidden behind generalities. In the end we may, as Paul said, only "see in a mirror, dimly." But that is better than closing one's eyes.

six

Making Meaningful Connections

A story is told about a prominent lay theologian who was something of an antiwar activist during the Vietnam War. In response to the question why he considered U.S. participation in the war to be unjustifiable, he is alleged to have exclaimed that the Vietnam War was wrong "because of the Resurrection." The story may only be apocryphal. But if he made such a statement, my hunch is that it left most of his listeners approximately where they were before they heard it. That would not have been reason enough for any supporter of U.S. policy to change his or her mind. At the same time, a serious moral objection to that or any other war could be mounted on the basis of a theology of resurrection, but much more would have to be said to make the connections between the theological doctrine and the policy implications clear. And when the full rationale was put forward, some find reason to say that other aspects of theology, combined with careful factual analysis, could lead to different conclusions.

A sermon, with the limitations imposed on it by time and the liturgical setting, does not allow for the complete analysis of any complex problem. But if a sermon is to be grounded theologically and relevant to an aspect of human existence, ways have to be found to make those connections clear and credible. If the sermon is done well, it will at least draw people into more serious thought about how their faith relates to life; it may additionally lead many to change their minds. Sometimes the connections may seem clear on the face of it; sometimes a good deal of thought may be required. But a meaningful connection can always be made between our faith and the problems we face. In this chapter I wish to suggest some possibilities.

God and the
Values We Hold

"You shall love the Lord your God with all your heart. . . ." That centerpoint in each of the biblical religions speaks directly, though broadly, to the values we hold. Our worship of God cannot be subordinated to any other human value. In one of his most perceptive books, H. Richard Niebuhr observed that what we worship as our "center of value" determines everything else.[7] Authentic Christian theology entails worship of the God who is the source of all being and goodness. Lesser forms include what he calls henotheism, the god of the tribe (or family, or nation, or any other human grouping), and polytheism, the worship of a variety of centers of value simultaneously. Most people are at least drawn toward some form of worship that is less than the worship of the One who is the source of all.

The next questions are, of course, who *is* this God? What is this God like? And what does this God require? These questions move us into deeper aspects of faith, including the affirmation that God is revealed in Christ. We may not be able to supply all the details. In fact, we surely will *not* be able to supply all the details concerning the nature and purposes of God. If we could, we would be on the same plane as God, and we are not. Nevertheless, even the affirmation that we are to worship the one God and no other suggests an important connection point for preaching. Whenever human values of any kind are worshiped in place of the one God, the prophetic point becomes very clear: Every lesser value is false when it is treated as if it were God.

Augustine makes the point in his classic distinction between the "city of God" and the earthly city. The city of God, he writes, is comprised of those who love God even to the point of being in contempt of themselves. The earthly city is made up of those who love themselves even to the point of being in contempt of God. We are, in any human culture, constantly challenged by inordinate love of limited goods. When patriotism, or "family values," or material consumption, or sex, or aesthetic tastes, or any other limited good is taken to be absolute, it has become a cultural idol in need of criticism for the sake of our true spiritual being. I do not think contemporary Western culture is necessarily more prone to idolatry than other past or present cultures, but there certainly are many idolatries in our time.

The interesting thing about idolatries is that very often they center on goods that really are good. Surely the family, the nation, aesthetic values, and other such values can be affirmed. The problem occurs when they are treated as absolutes, worthy of our unqualified devotion. Then they become idolatrous. Preaching must, from time to time, name the idols and put them in their place.

God's Love for People

Of course, the God of the Bible is not an abstract Being. The biblical narrative is about the revelation of God as God interacts with the people of Israel and, in the New Testament, the earliest Christians. And what emerges in that story, loud and clear, is God's boundless love. God continues to love humankind despite the most unspeakable forms of sin and rebellion. For Christians, that love is revealed with ultimate force by the sacrificial love of Christ on the cross. We are invited through that love to respond to God and to love one another.

Love does not automatically establish all the connecting points for us, partly because biblical love is more commitment than sentiment and partly because it is not always easy to express love intelligently. But the love of God—and our response of love for one another—does at least establish a crucial connection point: We have to pay serious attention to how things affect people.

A sermon on a social issue—such as poverty, or crime, or war—does well to bring things to life with vivid illustrations from the lives of real people who suffer in ways that others can be made to feel. Martin Luther King's word picture of his daughter's personal encounter with segregation helps us see just how evil that system really was:

> [W]hen you suddenly find your tongue twisted and your speech stammering as you seek to explain to your six-year-old daughter why she can't go to the public amusement park that has just been advertised on television, and see tears welling up in her little eyes when she is told that Funtown is closed to colored children, and see the depressing clouds of inferiority begin to form in her little mental sky, and see her begin to distort her little personality by unconsciously developing a bitterness toward white people . . . then you will understand why we find it difficult to wait.[8]

Is it honest to use this kind of anecdotal evidence in a sermon? Former President Ronald Reagan was sometimes criticized for exactly that as he used brief stories or anecdotes about people to embellish his speeches (for example, a "welfare queen" fraudulently living well off public welfare support). There is no question that the technique was very effective; there is some room for doubt about the honesty of using some of the stories. The question of honesty in the use of anecdotes is, of course, whether the illustrative story truly illustrates a much larger reality or whether it is an exception. To preach with integrity, one must take pains to learn more about the larger reality, just as one draws from the greater picture the particularly poignant human story that will help it come alive to people who have not yet experienced it. This certainly is better than a bare recital of statistics.

Nevertheless, there can be a place for both in the same sermon. For example, first can come a few pieces of statistical data followed by the question, What does this mean in human terms? And then a story or two. Or a sermon could begin with a poignant story or two followed by the question, Do you think these are just one or two isolated instances? Consider these facts. . . .

The stories of human suffering can easily be followed by some straight theology: How it must grieve the God who loves us and intends the fulfillment of each of us to witness such wretchedness! How it must grieve God to confront our hardness of heart! There is also a place in sermons to contrast human hurt with individual acts of love by caring people and with institutions and policies, the effects of which have been very good. In either case, the focus is upon what actually happens to real people.

Bringing the human reality to the fore does not always tell us what should be done. Even among the best-intentioned people there is often need for a good deal of factual experience and expertise. There is nothing wrong with a sermon acknowledging that there is room for honest disagreement among persons of goodwill. These disagreements have to do with what are the best means to good ends. When such disagreements surface, Christians must struggle with the question of what will *really* work to foster human good and alleviate suffering and tragedy. The tests of this can be quite pragmatic as long as we are unambiguously clear about the centrality of love.

The Theology of Creation

All who venture to deal with real issues and problems in their preaching sooner or later must face the criticism that their sermons should be less "materialistic." The gospel is about spiritual matters, not worldly ones. Put aside the suspicion that those who object to such preaching are not often discernibly "spiritual." Their criticism is worthy of serious theological response. Better yet, the issue should be anticipated theologically in the preaching itself, and not only in response to criticism of the preaching. But how are we to make the connection between the spiritual and the material?

Theologically trained preachers will recall that this represents one of the oldest doctrinal questions and controversies in Christian history. Numbers of early Christians (including most notably Marcion and his followers) were offended by the idea that the physical world was actually intended and created by the God and Father of our Lord Jesus Christ. The response of others—whose views became the orthodox position—was framed around the doctrine of creation. The world (translate, the whole tangible universe) was *created* by the very God whom we find revealed in Jesus Christ. The creation narratives of the Old Testament are not about some other deity; they are about the very same God whom we worship through Christ.

But how, then, are we to deal with the contrast between the spirit and the world? The work of two twentieth-century theologians is suggestive. One is the monumental section on the doctrine of creation in Karl Barth's *Church Dogmatics*. Barth's theological formula of the doctrine of creation is summarized as "creation [is] the external basis of the covenant" and "the covenant [is] the internal basis of creation." He elaborates, in words that obviously need simplification for pulpit use:

> Creation is the external—and only the external—basis of the covenant. It can be said that it makes it technically possible; that it prepares and establishes the sphere in which the institution and history of the covenant takes place; that it makes possible the subject which is to be God's partner in this history, in short the nature which the grace of God is to adopt and to which it is to turn in this history.[9]

We can think of "creation" as everything that is objective and tangible, including the whole cosmos, the world of nature, our physical bodies, and institutional structures. These things are not, in themselves, the *meaning* of existence but they are its necessary *preconditions*. They are not the same thing as the spiritual life, but without such preconditions the spiritual life cannot exist.

A similar tack is suggested by Dietrich Bonhoeffer's concept of the "penultimate," which is everything that precedes the "ultimate" and makes it possible. The ultimate, for the Christian, is the justification of the sinner by grace alone. It is the full realization of our humanity in and through the unmerited and boundless love of God. But earthly conditions can help or hinder that realization, that justification by grace. Bonhoeffer's way of illustrating this is graphically clear:

> If, for example, a human life is deprived of the conditions which are proper to it, then the justification of such a life by grace and faith, if it is not rendered impossible, is at least seriously impeded. . . . The hungry man needs bread and the homeless man needs a roof; the dispossessed need justice and the lonely need fellowship;

the undisciplined need order and the slave needs freedom. To allow the hungry man to remain hungry would be blasphemy
against God and one's neighbour. . . .[10]

So, in answer to the old question whether we live by bread alone,
the answer remains no, we do not. But that is not enough of an
answer. We also cannot exist *without* bread. At least, all of God's
purposes for us in this created existence, in this world, are frustrated when we do not have the conditions necessary to such a
life. Again, it is not that the *conditions* of life in the spirit are the
same thing as life in the spirit, but they support and enable—or,
in their absence, they defeat or diminish. So material questions are
very important spiritually.

This may be easier to see in relation to those things that affect
our physical well-being. But, as the Bonhoeffer quotation suggests, it is also true of institutional and political questions. A slave
can be well fed and cared for but still diminished in spirit. The op-
pressions of an unjust order make it very difficult for people to be
what God has created them to be. On the other hand, a regime
of law in which human rights are respected and protected can be
a positive reinforcement of our spiritual life, even if no legal order can by itself assure a Christian spirituality. I have already cited,
in chapter 3, how Walter Rauschenbusch nicely summarized the
distinction between just and unjust social orders. His succinct
statement helps us see the connections between spirituality and
social structures:

> An unchristian social order can be known by the fact that it makes
> good men do bad things. It tempts, defeats, drains, and degrades,
> and leaves men stunted, cowed, and shamed in their manhood. A
> Christian social order makes bad men do good things. It sets high
> aims, steadies the vagrant impulses of the weak, trains the powers
> of the young, and is felt by all as an uplifting force which leaves
> them with the consciousness of a broader and nobler humanity as
> their years go on.[11]

There are objectionable features in that definition, including the
archaic male language and the triumphalist ring to the phrase
"Christian social order." Nevertheless, has he not made the right

connections between spiritual life and systemic structures? There surely is a sense in which an unjust social order can "make" good people do bad things, even as they go about their everyday lives with scarcely a thought about the moral consequences of their actions. Equally, a just social order can make us behave better and, as we do act more justly, foster healthier social interactions and therefore enable a healthier spiritual life.

But we must repeat: It is not that attention to the objective conditions of human existence is the same thing as life in the Spirit. It is that the conditions of our existence can either serve or obstruct such a life.

Naming the Evils

It follows from this that specific evils can be identified and named. Evil in general can be seen as anything that obstructs God's ultimate purposes. I want to offer two clarifications about evil, both of which are relevant to the way we preach about it.

First, all sin is, by definition, evil. But not all evil is an expression of sin. I am thinking especially of natural evil—for example, earthquakes, famines, diseases, unpreventable accidents in which people are hurt or killed before their time or are, in other ways, unable to be what God has created them to be. Sometimes these things are indeed preventable. Even the loss of life and property through earthquakes or volcanic eruptions or floods can sometimes be prevented by not placing buildings in areas of known risk or by enacting building codes that enforce structural safety. Similarly, environmental health risks can be diminished in a variety of ways we are beginning to attend to. When we neglect to do what we *could* do to alleviate natural evils, that surely *is* a form of sin!

The connections can surely be made. I recall a homiletical campaign my father undertook in a small town in the 1930s. Winchester, Ohio, did not have safe water. People drew their water from wells, and in those years the water sometimes became contaminated. On more than one occasion, my father had to bury a small child of the community who had succumbed to typhoid fever as a result of drinking this contaminated water. So he named the evil and goaded the community to take advantage of federal matching grants that had become available to help small towns develop water systems. Typhoid fever was the principal evil. I'm sure my father did not consider the disease to be a sin. But having named the evil and identified a way to deal with it, it would have been possible to speak of the failure to act as sin.

My second point concerning preaching about evil is that it is a mistake to label something as evil unless one can demonstrate that, in fact, it really *is* evil. Sometimes what we call "evil" is a very large, complex phenomenon in need of careful analysis. Often we need to spell out carefully the reasons *why* something is evil before we call it evil. Today a vast majority of Christians would unhesitatingly say that slavery is clearly evil—even though the Bible is not so clear about that and there are biblical writings admonishing slaves to be good servants (and masters to treat their slaves humanely, though not necessarily to release them!). In John Wesley's time it was necessary for Christians like him to spell out the reasons—as he and the Quakers and a few other antislavery Christians did. Today also a vast majority of Christians understand perfectly well that racial segregation is evil. But I can well recall a period when it was necessary in most parts of the country to explain *why*. A sermon on racial segregation today would be very different from one given in 1950.

There are Christians in our time who want to identify capitalism or military armaments or homophobia or exclusively masculine language for God as evils. But these things are all disputed. Whether they are evil, in whole or in part, has to be demonstrated; it cannot simply be assumed. It is a homiletical mistake simply to label something as evil if there are people out there who do not believe it to be evil. People have to be convinced; the connection has to be made. Sometimes the presently disputed issue will come to be seen as a clear evil, and then it can simply be named. Sometimes we may come to see that it is not, at least not intrinsically, evil; then we will move on to other things. Sometimes we may see that *aspects* of what we have named are evil. (I suspect we may have to speak of aspects or forms of capitalism and aspects of military armaments in that way and not to label such things as wholesale evils.)

If there is doubt about any of this, I would err on the side of giving the reasons. Does it weaken the force of the message to explain why it is true and why it matters? I do not think so. I suppose there may be a sense in which we weaken the condemnation of evil by implying that it is still a debatable matter. But one can develop the reasons for one's view without doing that. In fact, a reasoned discourse can be one way of saying why this should no longer be treated as debatable. We cannot bring closure to such a subject by treating it as a closed subject among people who have yet to be convinced.

The Tragedy of Sin

While not all evil is necessarily sin, all sin is necessarily evil. Sin is separation from God and from the good that could be. Is sin always a matter of deliberate choice? In one sense the answer to that may be yes, for one can scarcely be blamed for things one did not choose to do or for conditions one is powerless to avert. But the deeper truth is that we may be powerless to avert attitudes and behaviors that are destructive. Preaching about original sin can be more prophetic than simply identifying the particular sins that people commit, because it can reveal the inner spiritual condition that leads—sometimes almost inevitably—to the particulars. When the doctrine of original sin is put in abstract form, it makes almost no connection with real life experience. What can it possibly mean to people to be told that Adam sinned and we have inherited the guilt, from which we can only be released if we accept that Jesus paid the price, making it possible for God to accept us? Even a dispute over this substitutionary theory of the atonement can be strangely abstract, regardless of which side is "right," for its focus is often upon what Christ has done to satisfy God's abstract sense of justice. A better connection must be made between the doctrine and real-life experience, or the doctrine may remain one of those things we are only supposed to believe.

Reinhold Niebuhr's explication of original sin helps us see just how profound the doctrine is and how it connects with real-life experience.[12] According to Niebuhr, human spiritual life transcends the "temporal and natural process" in which we are involved. But that very fact brings awareness of our vulnerability. We can suffer; ultimately we will die. It is as though we can be teased by unlimited visions of the universe of time and space, yet know that our lives are destined to be snuffed out by cosmic forces to which we are absolutely meaningless. So we have to make our own meaning. In our anxiety we seek "to transmute . . . finiteness into infinity . . . weakness into strength . . . dependence into independence." That is the root cause of the particular sins, whether they be the sins of sensuality or of dominance. Through sin we seek to control what ultimately cannot be controlled. Seen in this light, a Napoleon or a Hitler is revealed in his deep spiritual weakness, not in the pretense with which he clothes himself.

Prophetic preaching can help people confront the reality and consequences of this anxiety of which Niebuhr speaks, demonstrating its relationship to self-destructive and other-destructive behavior. But that is not enough. Somehow we must come to a deeper level of trust. Until we can trust the One in whose hands our destiny lies, we will be given over to self-centered despair.

Is that too stark a portrait? Perhaps so, for even as we despair over our vulnerability we also experience, at least in human terms, the love that is the building block of trust. No conception of original sin that pictures human beings as *utterly* sinful will be faithful to the prevenient grace that is also a part of our experience. Still, until we can trust God's love in the very core of our being, we will sometimes, maybe often, do wicked things.

It remains the perennial work of preaching to identify the sins and their spiritual roots and call people to repentance. This will always be more effective when people are drawn to identify themselves in the picture: *This really is me. I really am doing destructive things to myself and to others. I don't have to because I can really trust God's love. I can find the greater human fulfillment as I respond with love.*

The temptation of preaching is to remain at a more generalized spiritual level, and our preaching must surely be as deep as we can make it. But if the connections are to be made we must also develop skills in rational discernment of moral issues. We know that we were made to worship God and to love one another; we know the roots of the sin that deflects us toward destructiveness. But how can we know that particular things really *are* sins or evils and how best to avoid them? And how can we identify the good in the complexities of human existence? To speak to such things, the pulpit must feed the mind as well as the spirit. I wish, in the following chapter, to discuss that dimension of our preaching more specifically.

seven

Preaching for Perspective

I have already made the point that prophetic preaching must be theological before it is ideological. Basic values come from the center of our faith, not from portraits of the world as it is or as we (for nontheological reasons) want it to be. Nevertheless, if our preaching is to make sense about the real world, it helps to have a broad picture of major aspects of life. For instance, what is involved in the realm of politics? What is at stake? Why does it matter? Preaching can sometimes attempt to lay out such road maps to help people understand their existence in the light of their faith. I believe that ought to be done occasionally—not frequently, but often enough to help people think broadly. Even when preaching does not venture the whole picture, it must presuppose broad perspectives. In this chapter I wish to consider four broad areas of human existence—politics, economics, racial and ethnic issues, and the family.

Perspectives on Politics

Whenever people object to sermons dealing with social issues, they are likely to frame this in terms of keeping politics out of the pulpit or not "mixing" religion and politics.[13] Sometimes, indeed, it is alleged that in the United States it is *illegal* to preach on politics. The reference there is to the First Amendment to the U.S. Constitution that prohibits Congress from passing laws "respecting an establishment of religion." From that and similar state laws, it is clear that the state is not in the religion business. Tax money cannot be used directly to support religious bodies. Reference can also be made to specific laws at federal and local levels that exempt religious organizations from paying taxes and allow donors to such organizations to claim their contributions as tax deductions. The First Amendment, if anything, guarantees the freedom to speak on political subjects (or any other subjects upon which one's religious faith impacts). The tax laws, which do not provide exemptions for political organizations and contributions, do mean that religious bodies cannot behave as political parties if they wish to preserve their privileged tax status. That is normally taken to apply to interventions in political campaigns. It is not taken to prohibit purely educational activities or taking positions on public policy *issues* (in contrast to candidates and parties). So we can be clear that the pulpit is perfectly free to deal with issues, but it had better be circumspect about endorsing candidates or parties. I believe this distinction is a wise one to adhere to, regardless of questions of law.

But then we must ask, What is politics? I wish to make two points about this. First, politics involves the actions of society as a whole. The political struggle is over the policies and laws to be adopted by all of us when we act in concert and over which leaders or representatives will be entrusted with power to act on behalf of the whole community. Does this mean that the realm of politics presupposes universal *agreement* on policies, laws, and leadership? Of course not; that would be impossible anywhere. It does mean that those who disagree with public policy and its leadership *acquiesce* in it. At any moment, there are many laws and policies of federal and local government with which I am in hearty disagreement. But since I respect the legitimacy of the political order, I do not leave the country or act in rebellion against it. I continue to pay my taxes, which provide the resources to be used by the state. If I did not, the tax authorities would attach my income. If I did not have enough income to pay taxes, any form of economic activity in which I engaged would still contribute to the resource base enabling the state to act. I am, in effect, doing whatever the state is doing, like it or not.

The broad perspectival point to be derived from this is that

Christians do not have the option of retreating from the state. There is no zone of purity to which we can repair in order to avoid the contamination of the moral evils of the public order. We are implicated up to our eyebrows. Thus, sermons on social issues speak to people as actors in the public sphere, not as spectators only. Many people don't want to be actors, but they are anyway. The only question is whether in their acting they will act in accordance with their faith.

The other point about politics is that, as a form of power, it is most fundamentally the power of influence. In politics, people act as agents. They choose to do something—or to avoid doing something—and then they do it—or don't do it. It is their choice. Even when exercised unconsciously or involuntarily, it is their *will* to do or not do that counts. Sometimes we say that people are "forced" to act in particular ways. It may appear so. But physical force is politically relevant only to the extent it influences the will. (I must acknowledge that I, personally, am easily influenced by the prospect of pain! I do not know how I would behave in a coercive state. I suspect I would be too easily terrorized. I hope not, but the history of such states suggests that most people will acquiesce in order to avoid fearful consequences.) Physical force can be most persuasive, but there have been numbers of people, known and unknown to history, who have resisted. In the end they could be killed or buried away in prison, but they could not be "forced" to do or say what they would not.

The broad meaning of this is that anything that *does* influence our will is at least potentially political. We act in accordance with our values—which may be economic, social, familial, or simply the insurance of survival. Religion, as repository of ultimate values, is definitely politicizable. The actual role of religion has varied through history. In our own time, the Middle East, Ireland, Bosnia, and the Bible Belt of the United States all illustrate the considerable influence of religion in politics. Sometimes we may feel that religion has played an important and prophetic role. Sometimes we deplore the narrowness religion has inflicted upon the state. But religion, when taken seriously, will definitely be important in politics.

How should this affect our preaching? Prophetic preaching, at least as envisioned by this book, will avoid narrow appeals to religion in politics. In fact, it will seek to inoculate people against the wrong kinds of religious political influence. People need to be warned against religious demagoguery in politics, first because of its religious idolatries and second because of its effects in distorting the political process. Not everything that pretends to be religious is. The wolf often travels in sheep's clothing. Religious people must be especially leery of the promise that their particular form of religion will be given special preference in the competition of religious bodies. In the end—religious people should know this better than anybody else—the only victories that matter in the cultural sphere are those gained by persuasion. External enhancements can, if anything, diminish the real authority of religion. When religious institutions are wedded to political power and there is great advantage to be had from being identified with those institutions, how can one tell who is really committed and who is not?

Occasionally the pulpit should be used to teach about such things. There was an interesting custom in some states in the early years of this republic called the "election sermon."[14] The sermon, preached at election time, was not intended to instruct the congregation to vote for particular candidates. Rather, it was to underscore the importance of elections, the civic responsibility of voters, and the seriousness of public service. I rather like the idea, and every two years, as a congressional or presidential election approaches, I preach on the central importance of politics. Sometimes the focus will be on the vocation of citizenship and public service, sometimes on issues that have come to the fore in the campaign. I do not believe it is the proper function of such sermons to take sides or even to lean one way or another. But an election sermon can help people see the connections between their faith and a major aspect of their lives; occasionally it can contribute to the public debate itself. A sermon of this kind probably should not be preached two days before the election, but neither should it be so far in advance that people are not yet focused on the campaign.

Perspectives on Economics

If politics is central to human life, economics may be even more so. And yet I believe most preachers are sincerely afraid of economics. It is not because they consider it unimportant and not because they no longer consider the vast amount of biblical attention given the subject to be applicable. I think it is because they feel so incompetent, in face of the expertise of economists and businesspeople. Armed with their mathematical models and statistical jargon, economists can be intimidating. Businesspeople, having run the risks and met the payrolls, can be intimidating in another way: They are the ones who know what works. What, given the intellectual expertise of the economists and the practical experience of the successful businessperson, does the preacher have to add? Isn't it better to leave economics to the experts?

It might seem so. But in this, as in other areas of life experience, preachers and theologians and ethicists can help people see why it matters—and, on the basis of why it matters, to see where the real problems lie. In this, curiously enough, a preacher can be the truly pragmatic participant in discussions of economic issues. Pragmatism is concerned about what works. But what works has to do with ends, not only with means. A given set of business policies (including, maybe, corporate downsizing and hostile takeovers) may make some businesspersons wealthy. That, to them, might seem quite pragmatic. But those who lose their jobs do not share this view. A given set of economic policies might greatly increase the gross national product of a nation's economy. But if the wealth is poorly distributed, what is good for the nation might not necessarily be good for all of its people. Pragmatic policies are not to be judged on the basis, simply, of "what works" but, rather, "what works for good purposes." The focus in economic life should be on what works for everyone, for the community as a whole, and, in the larger theological perspective, what works to advance God's purposes on earth. Technical expertise alone cannot supply answers to the ultimate value questions.

What are those questions as they apply to economics? I wish to suggest five.[15]

The first is the most obvious: Is there enough production of the necessities of life to provide for everybody? The distribution of resources is crucial too, of course, and people who are most concerned about economic justice tend to emphasize that. But one must start with actual production, without which even the most ideal system of distribution has nothing to distribute. The socialist Michael Harrington once observed that you cannot socialize poverty.[16] Faced with the alternatives of equality without prosperity and prosperity without equality, people have a tendency to choose the latter with distressing regularity! Economics must therefore be concerned about inventive creativity, raw materials, adequate transportation and communication facilities, energy sources, and a sufficiently trained and motivated workforce. The United States is such an incredibly productive country that we are likely to take these things for granted. It is not so everywhere. From the Ireland of the potato famine to the marginal life of many in contemporary Bangladesh, the sheer insufficiency of material goods has blighted every other aspect of human life. Production is important enough that a good deal of human effort must be devoted to it in any society. It is an important part of the spiritual vocation for, as many Christian thinkers from the time of Luther have understood, work devoted to the meeting of material needs can be as seriously spiritual as the more explicitly religious vocations. This does not mean that we fulfill our complete humanity on the material level. We do not live by bread alone. But bread is a necessary condition for everything else in this earthly existence of ours.

The second important economic question is: Is the distribution of goods and services equitable? The word "equitable" is admittedly a weasel word. It suggests equality, but it does not exactly mean equality. It means a distribution that is fair, but what is "fair"? To the medieval mind, fairness meant an allocation of goods to people in ways appropriate to their more or less fixed station in life. By contrast, contemporary economic thought often suggests that we are entitled to what we can earn (or inherit) under free market conditions. That doctrine of laissez-faire capitalism feeds the complacency of the wealthy, talented, and lucky members of society. It suggests an attitude toward society that is highly individualistic and competitive and hardly consonant with the biblical perspective.

Neither the medieval nor the modern market-oriented conception of equity is quite up to the mark. Although absolute equality is difficult to conceive, much less attain, in a world of such diverse needs and interests, "equity" can be taken to mean a form of distribution that best enables all to participate together in the life of community. Differences of income and wealth can be so great as to strain our sense of fellow humanity. The underlying question, to be put to every economic policy or program, is: What effect will it really have on the realization of community?

The third economic question is: Does the economic system provide for full employment and educational opportunity? We think of work as the means of livelihood, which in the main it is. But even those who have no need for livelihood still have the need to work—if work is considered broadly to be putting forth effort to serve others. Indeed, some of the things that are really "work" do not always provide income in market terms. (Consider the starving artist, for instance—or many "unemployed" mothers, for that matter.) Unemployment can be a tragedy of wasted lives and eroded self-esteem.[17] We all need to feel that we have something to contribute. In a dynamic economy, full employment does not literally mean everybody working. A certain percentage of the potential workforce (perhaps two or three percent) will be looking for their first jobs or temporarily between jobs. There is, however, a pernicious and questionable economic doctrine (related to what economists call the Phillips curve) that holds that a somewhat higher level of unemployment is necessary in order to keep the rate of inflation in check. The theory is that, with full employment, employers have to compete for workers, thus driving the wages higher and higher in an inflationary spiral. Recent U.S. economic experience—and experience in this country and elsewhere in other periods—calls that into question. Even if it were so, would the implication be that numbers of people must be sacrificed economically for the sake of the rest?

Along with employment opportunity, we cite the importance of education. Actually, educational opportunity is absolutely essential to economic performance in a dynamic economy, quite apart from the role of education in the fulfillment of our human potentialities. I list educational opportunity under economics because in a real sense it is an economic activity. It is one that an enlightened society provides for all its young citizens—even requiring all to participate. But it is more than a matter of economics. It is preparation for full participation in the cultural and political life of the community. A high-quality education is one of the best guarantors of social mobility, helping to ensure that social inequalities will not be frozen along caste lines.

The fourth question is: Will these economic policies and practices be good for the planet and good for the long haul? Economic life sometimes imposes harsh dilemmas as we are forced to choose between short-term economic necessity and long-term environmental conservation. One thinks of Brazilian rain forests being cleared to provide jobs for more people, adversely affecting the soil and even the earth's atmosphere. Or desperately poor people in Bangladesh cutting down trees for needed firewood, contributing thereby to the erosion of soil in the highlands and devastating floods. If economic necessity fosters such dilemmas, economic creativity may be needed to resolve them. Environmental pessimists can point to a good deal of ruinous economic behavior in the past as the industrial revolution has taken hold around the world. But technology can help us conserve as well as destroy. The development of transistors and microchips, vastly increasing capacity for information transmission while actually decreasing energy requirements, illustrates the point. The U.S. auto industry, under severe public and legal pressure, demonstrated that more fuel-efficient and pollution-free internal combustion engines can be developed. More and more cities are developing less-polluting rapid transit systems. Even the space program, for all its wastefulness in other ways, has helped us develop more energy-efficient ways of accomplishing economic objectives.

It remains to be seen whether these beneficent possibilities will be enough to offset the environmental damages of the industrial epoch. It is a question that needs to be pressed from the pulpit, for it engages us with the deepest problems of stewardship that humanity as a whole has ever had to face. Will we, in fact, be able to preserve this beautiful world and enhance its God-given potentialities? Or will we turn it into a lifeless desert like the moon and Mars?

It is sobering to consider just how fast things have moved, economically, in the past two centuries. On the one hand we can marvel at the extraordinary inventiveness of the human community. On the other hand we can be appalled at the damage inflicted upon the world and the risks the world is running. I do not believe the pulpit has the expertise to resolve environmental questions; isn't it cause for concern that nobody else has the expertise we need either? In addressing such questions, the pulpit can urge caution in face of the unknown. Better to be conservative about risk-taking when the potential risks can be so great. And the pulpit can help to stimulate a more serious dialogue in which many kinds of expertise can be shared.

The fifth question is: Will the directions of economic development help in the further realization of world community? Viewed in theological perspective, it is difficult to see how we can restrict our concerns to our own country. In the long run, that is probably true of sound economics as well. The economic principle of comparative advantage emphasizes the economic benefits to all from maximizing trade. As the quickening of world trade draws more and more societies into its orbit, the economic development of neglected areas is enhanced and everybody benefits. That is at least true in theory and often in practice. In real-world economics, we know that the terms of trade can matter. At the national level we have learned, often the hard way, that regulation of the free market can be very important for the sake of fair labor standards, environmental protection, protection for consumers, and the avoidance of too-great concentrations of economic power in too-few hands. Regulation, in face of powerful economic interests, can be very difficult at the national level. It is even more daunting at the global level.

We will have to struggle with the implications of this for some time to come. The emerging shape of a truly global economy is far too important to ignore; it is far too difficult for us to pretend to have easy answers. I do believe that the prophetic vision of a world economic order must continue to emphasize that God's agenda is the whole world, not just our own country—and it emphasizes concern for the well-being of even the humblest of people everywhere.

During the 1970s, Latin American liberation theologians often spoke of God's "preferential option for the poor." The term, awkward as it is when translated from Spanish into English, reminds us that the weakest links in the chain of humanity are the ones who must claim our most serious attention. It is not that the poor are any better than anyone else or more loved by God. It is that, for the sake of the whole human community, these are the ones whose condition most urgently requires our attention. They draw us back to the Bible, with its deep and persistent concern for the poor. Modern economic complexities challenge us as we seek to translate that concern into effective policies.

Racial and Ethnic Tensions

Most Americans have grown up in a society that is still so affected by the virus of racism that it is difficult to think very clearly about race. For example, it is difficult to grasp the fact that there is no such thing. At least, there is no such thing as *biological* race. Is that so? What could be plainer than racial differences? Who, if not vision-impaired, can fail to see the differences?

The question that racism obscures is one that ought to be obvious: Which differences matter when we define race? My wife had an experience several years ago that helps to illuminate the point. Traveling for the first time in Ireland, she looked about her at the Dublin airport. There, she later exclaimed to her bemused husband, "I suddenly felt that I was with my own kind!" Perhaps you have guessed why. She is a redhead, and everywhere she looked in Ireland there were redheads!

In the nineteenth- and twentieth-century literature on racial classification, I do not know of any that defines redheads as a "race." And yet if there were sociological reasons for doing so it would be done. Is that a fair illustration? Don't those groups that historically have been classified as "races" share many more characteristics than hair color? Don't races present us with a bundle of shared biological features: skin color, facial configurations, hair texture, and the like? Perhaps. But genetic study makes clear that the genes responsible for each of the identifiable features are independent of the rest. An illustration of the point: There are many Indians (from India) whose skin color is darker—even much darker—than many Africans or African Americans, but whose hair and facial features are more similar to Europeans. How are they to be defined? There are "white" people with very different kinds of hair and facial characteristics. And none of these external physiological characteristics correlates with intelligence—for that matter, intelligence itself takes a variety of forms.

"Race" is sociological, cultural, and historical in ways that are more important than the biological. Any gene pool, developed over a long period of time, will evince a broad "package" of similarities, most of which are comprehensible effects of climate and other environmental factors. But the choice of which packages are to be defined as races grows out of social, not biological, experience. Why, for instance, is skin color taken to be more important than physical size? Gene pools tend toward similarities of stature. One notes that people in some parts of Africa were unusually short while people in other parts were unusually tall. That was not important in defining race because it was Africa as a whole that had to be categorized—for sociological, not biological, reasons. Adolf Hitler, archracist that he was, could identify himself with the Aryans he prized so much, even though he was not a tall, blue-eyed, blond Scandinavian! In the ebb and flow of intergroup relations, there has often been enough shared physiological appearance in the "other" group to help tag it for animosity or disdain and oppression.

What then of racial identity? It is a consciousness of "kind," marking those with whom one shares selected physiological traits as the most significant social grouping. If one's group, thus selected, has the upper hand in society, it provides a basis for self-worth and a justification for the mistreatment of others. If one is part of a racially oppressed group, the identity is one of shared experience, especially of shared suffering. Cultural differences grow up around these forms of group identity; thus, the externally visible forms of identification are reinforced by different ways of acting, even of thinking. My wife was kidding about her identity as a redhead. In society at large, racial identity can be deadly serious.

What are we to make of it theologically? Naive racism (all racism is naive) developed its theological justifications. I recall how shocked I was in doing research on the history of racial segregation in my denomination to discover that one of its most prominent theologians announced to the church's General Conference in 1936 that God made the races separate and intended for them to remain that way. The theologian offered that as justification for creation of a separate administrative structure for the African Americans in the church.

That was bad sociology. It was even worse theology. For when we treat "race" as ground for separation or for superior social status, we are imputing a value to external characteristics and thereby subordinating the human characteristics that really matter. The plain theological term for this is idolatry. One has elevated a relative and superficial thing to ultimate status.

Isn't it far better to see the glory of God shining through so many different forms of biological and cultural humanity and to regard human diversity not as an obstacle to the fulfillment of God's intended community on earth but as an extraordinary gift for the enhancement of community?

How painful it is for a society with a long history of racism to come to that realization. Most of the racial dilemmas faced by contemporary America have their origin there. For some years America has struggled with the issue of what has been called affirmative action—whether special efforts should be made to ensure opportunity for groups with a history of oppression. The central dilemma is easy enough to state but very hard to address creatively: When a group is singled out for special consideration in order to overcome prejudice, this reinforces the very group separations we are hoping to break down. Put differently, it is difficult to emphasize the universal human values if we base social policy on inherited group differences. Why not just forget the group labels and focus on individual gifts and needs? Moreover, when a member of a previously subjugated group receives an opportunity (in education, employment, leadership), the suspicion lingers that but for the fact of being a member of the particular group this person would not be there. Partly for that reason, some minority group members strongly oppose affirmative action.

But, on the other hand, affirmative action has undeniably made a big difference in moving things along, in education, the military, business, churches. Without special efforts could it have happened? It was never just a matter of helping minority group persons and women overcome their inadequacies, quite the reverse; it was helping the majority overcome *its* inadequacies! Without the pressure of affirmative action, it has been all too easy for a majority to settle for a familiar mediocrity. That is palpably true of American athletics; it is also true of other spheres of American life, as the truly outstanding contributions of women and people of racial and ethnic minority groups have made clear.

We have to preach about such things, unpopular though the message may be in some quarters. At the same time, we must acknowledge the reality of the dilemmas. I wish more Americans could see this as historical process, to be worked at with patience and a willingness to experiment. Theological perspective can help us here. We do not have to have fixed and "principled" solutions based more on ideology than on a deeper sense of what is ultimately at stake.

Perspectives on Family Life

I wish to comment, finally, on the family. So much has been said and written in recent years about "family values" that one hesitates to try to say more. It is the one area where the pulpit's right to speak is virtually uncontested—provided the right things are said, of course. Family and religion have always been understood to be deeply intertwined. It is easy to see why. The family is the most basic nurturing unit of our humanity. It is the place where our most basic values are formed. Sociologists remind us that we tend to take on the values of the individuals and groups whose approval we most seek. Many people have had very damaging family experiences, but for most people—at least in the formative years—the family is the group whose values, often unconsciously, we assimilate.

From a sociological perspective, there are, of course, many different forms of family unit. Regardless of form, most families are settings in which people are known, more or less, as whole persons. Ideally, families are settings in which people find acceptance despite their flaws and idiosyncracies. The family is the place to which one can repair when rejected elsewhere. As Robert Frost put it, "home is where, when you have to go there, they have to take you in." That isn't always the way it works. The intimacies of family life create a paradox. When you are accepted there, it can be wonderfully humanizing. But when you are rejected by your family, that is the most devastating loss. One must take most seriously whether one is accepted or rejected by those who know one best.

If the doctrine of God's grace is at or close to the center of Christian faith, the importance of this nurturing role of the family can scarcely be overstated. The family, by nurturing love or fostering alienation and rejection, helps determine whether a person is capable of trusting the love of God. God's love is not abstract belief. It is experienced most of all in human form. Those for whom family life has been damaging have very little basis upon which to draw positive conclusions about God. Those who have experienced dependable, accepting love are far better prepared to see this as a manifestation of the deeper love of God. The character of the family is just that important.

This has obvious implications for the raising of children. Children need most of all the time, attention, and love of committed caregivers. No parents or other caregivers are perfect, and styles of acceptable parenting vary greatly. The worst problems of parenting often result from the parents' own earlier experiences of having been neglected or abused. It is not easy to break the generational cycles. It is certainly important for the church to be as solid a resource as it can be for healthy family life. Sometimes, even in a large church, it is possible for others to share the burdens of caregiving with the primary caregivers. In quiet ways, those who have more experience can help provide role models and encouragement to those with less experience.

Most families begin with the marriage of those who are to become parents. The deep commitment of love begins there, in the marriage, before it is bestowed on the children. Regardless of the words used in the wedding liturgy, the reality of marriage is lifelong commitment. In my own denominational tradition, the liturgy consciously builds on the analogy of God's unqualified love. Just as God, in Christ, is committed to us, so are husband and wife committed to each other. At one point in the liturgy, the covenant of marriage is described as representing the covenant between Christ and his church. The point is not that one partner is Christ and the other the church; the point is that both partners are to be grace to each other, as Christ is grace to the church. Nobody can perfectly fulfill that. But the bond is understood in just such serious terms.

Many denominations have come to see divorce as a sometime necessity, particularly in situations that are abusive beyond remedy. But divorce is always a very sad thing. It is about something once embraced as good that has now come to represent not the enhancement of human values but their destruction. Where children are involved, it can be particularly tragic. Sometimes it is said that divorce is better for the children, and sometimes that is so. But one must take serious note of the testimony of the children of divorced parents who often, years later, fantasize the reunion of their mother and father. I find it interesting that divorced parents consider the relationship with their children to be an absolute given. The Christian conception of marriage views the marriage bond in like terms.

The churches once held to this view so inflexibly that the commitment took on a legalistic character remote from the grace it was supposed to embody. We do not want to return to that! Nor do we want to heap judgment upon those who, having been divorced or having found themselves in quite intolerable marriages, cannot be to one another what marriage means. The best way to teach grace is to *be* grace. And if the church would heal the brokenness of those who have experienced failure in marriage, it must first of all be grace to them. But the church is the place where people can be prepared for healthy marriage and where many can find healing *within* their marriages—not *from* their marriages.

I have spoken of family life and marriage in more or less traditional terms. It must now be acknowledged that family life, in the deepest moral sense, is not restricted to those terms. Here, for example, is a middle-aged woman who has not found a mate but has always longed to be a mother. She adopts a young child from an orphanage in another country. They get along fabulously well. She is a natural as a mother. She and her child are, to each other, what family means. Here is a gay couple who have been committed to each other faithfully and monogamously for many years. Some who speak most loudly about "family values" in our society consider this a threat to family life. But is it really? Is family not to be judged (if judgment is called for) by the quality of love and commitment? Here is a group of nuns, living together in a convent near the school where they teach. They are not a family in any traditional sense. And yet, in a moral and spiritual sense, perhaps they are. And perhaps they manage to incorporate something of the reality of family life into their relationship with the occasional child in their school who has been neglected by his or her family of origin. The point is, we all need that circle of deep affection and commitment, and if it is not a possibility in traditional terms there may be other forms. Jesus himself, in one of those hard sayings of scripture, speaks of those who do the will of his Father as being his parent and brothers. The will of God is love.

Another point must be added. Inherited traditions of family organization have throughout most of history relegated women to subservient status. That is so, even in cultures inclined to place wives and mothers on a pedestal, for the pedestal is beyond the reach of real participation as an equal partner in marriage. The culture is struggling with this. I do not wonder that the changes of gender role expectations should be so unsettling and give rise to such irrational backlashes. In respect to this, as to all deep social change, the church should strive for that elusive combination of grace with persistence. In this, the pulpit can play a very substantial role—particularly if substantial numbers of women also occupy pulpits!

eight

The Art of
Prophetic Preaching

I wince a little every time I hear preaching referred to as an art. That can suggest a style of preaching that places a greater premium upon the sheer beauty of the imagery or the cleverness of alliteration than it does upon the gospel message itself. Or it can suggest a manipulative use of rhetorical devices rather than the plain truth. In particular, what can art have to do with *prophetic* preaching? Surely an inelegant expression of truth is better than a beautifully expressed falsehood, and even a beautifully expressed truth can be diminished, subtly, if the style upstages the substance.

Even so, great truth can be enhanced by its packaging. Otherwise, would we be so deeply affected by insightful poetry, penetrating novels, and great drama? There truly is an art to preaching. Like other art forms, it is difficult to reduce it to a set of principles. Different preachers, like different poets or dramatists or composers, put their own unique stamp on their work. In some respects the art of preaching is among the most difficult of all, for the preacher (unlike most musicians or dramatists) must both "compose" the work and "perform" it—and most preachers must do this week after week! No wonder that even the finest preachers are not at their best every week, try as they must, and that even mediocre preachers can sometimes deliver an outstanding sermon.

In what follows, I do not attempt a rounded discussion of the art of preaching. Others have done that better than I could, and it is not what this book is about anyway. I do wish to suggest several principles that can enhance our words when we venture to preach prophetically.

Principle One:
Speak to the Listeners

It is easy to forget that the sermon that counts is not the one that is written but the one that is heard. As Fred Craddock puts it, "The goal is not to get something said but to get something heard."[18] It is very important to know (or, better yet, to feel) the mood and state of mind of the congregation.

If the congregation is already deeply moved—by a tragedy, an injustice, a common peril, a situation of historic proportions—it is not necessary to introduce the element of drama. It is already there. In such a climate the most artful speech is often the simplest. Lincoln's Gettysburg Address would not have roused an apathetic audience, but his listeners were gripped by crisis and tragedy. In that setting, simple words about the meaning of the struggle were eloquent. Not that there was no art involved. The address was most carefully honed until every word was exactly right. But in such a context, the speaker could count on each of those words resonating—no need for a story to "warm up" the audience! His predecessor at the platform, Edward Everett, gave a standard two-hour nineteenth-century oration. I have read only excerpts from it, but I wonder whether he thought he had to create a mood when the mood was already there.

On the other hand, an apathetic or complacent audience does need to be stimulated. Here a compelling story or engaging humor can establish contact and interest. Better to do it quickly, too, before the eyes glaze over entirely.

The importance of the congregation's mood was borne in upon me one Easter. Often the mood of Easter is already so upbeat that one does not have to create interest (although it is also true that the rustling of an Easter congregation, with a multitude of distractions, can create a focusing problem for the preacher). This particular Easter I had prepared an introduction to the sermon that was full of the mood of joyous triumph, and I planned to work from that into a message that would leave the congregation with a greater sense of the meaning of resurrection faith. The New Testament lesson had just been read when a loud, threatening voice came down from the crowded balcony. The tone was so violent that people expected some awful act to follow. The congregation was terrorized; you could feel it. It ended quickly enough. As the young man was ushered out, I spoke quietly to the congregation about how this was obviously a troubled person in need of our prayers and that each of us should pray for him before we left the sanctuary. The choir was then to sing a "gradual," the anthem preceding the sermon. I had that long to come up with a very different entry into my sermon. Instead of the note of Easter triumph, I began by speaking of the disciples' fear and discouragement that first Easter morning before it came to them what God was really doing. It was as though all the brokenness and hurt of the world lay on their shoulders. We must understand that the great victory of Easter is brought home to us in exactly those moments when we have been most fearful and depressed. And then I gradually moved the sermon back onto the originally planned track. It seems clear to me that a failure to respond to the congregation's mood would have been a homiletical disaster.

Principle Two: Establish the Legitimacy of Preaching on Controversial Issues

The letter I quoted at the beginning of chapter 5 clearly illustrates that there are people who do not just disagree with what is said on specific controversial issues from the pulpit. They consider it wrong to say *anything* on such subjects in sermons. But preaching is not just to make people feel good. At stake is not just prophetic preaching but *any* real preaching, and the deeper question is not just about real preaching but about real worship. Worship, including preaching, cannot be authentic if it is nothing more than a projection of what we already believe. And preaching that cannot be applied to the real circumstances of life will not help a congregation relate faith to life.

When that point is not already understood and accepted by a

congregation, it is well for a preacher to deal with the problem from the pulpit. But I believe it best to deal with the question of the appropriateness of preaching on controversial issues at a time when the congregation is not caught up in the passions of some particular issue. The principle that preachers should be free—even expected—to deal with the issues of the day in light of the gospel can best be absorbed by a congregation that is not at that moment also dealing with an inflamed issue of the day. Illustrations can be drawn from the history of preaching—including, of course, biblical illustrations. This can be identified as a very important part of our heritage, without which we could not be what we are. We can honor those who paid a price to preach the "truth in love," with illustrations drawn from the preaching of those who were clearly right—as seen in contemporary perspective: for instance, those who raised their voices against slavery or the torturing of heretics or the subordination of women. Such a sermon can acknowledge and illustrate how sometimes prophetic preachers have been wrong about particular issues and how, even when wrong, their courage and devotion to truth has made a contribution to the tradition.

I believe it is well to preach about one's understanding of preaching fairly early in a pastorate. Then people will not be as surprised later, when the preacher feels it important to deal with particular controversial issues from the pulpit. They may still disagree, but they will be less likely to consider such preaching inappropriate.

Principle Three:
Appeal to Values Held in Common

Earlier I made the point that appeal to shared values is important in communication. That is especially so in treating controversial issues. One reason why issues are controversial is that they really express larger conflicts over value questions. The abortion question, for instance, is so inflamed because it involves so many other issues of family life and gender role. Establishing a good deal of common ground with an audience or congregation can be very important in gaining a hearing at points of difference. Obviously, in preaching, one reaches for the deepest values, the ultimate loyalties, that bind us together as a community of faith. One seeks to express the faith—in God, in Christ, in scripture—in terms that will be recognizable to the congregation, even while leading the congregation toward deeper interpretations of familiar landmarks. The more controversial the point of application, the more important it is to be grounded in common faith.

While the ultimate loyalties are far the most important, establishing common ground on subordinate values can be helpful as well—to the extent this can be done with integrity. One would not appeal to racist values as a way of establishing common ground with a racist audience, no matter what rhetorical objective that might achieve! But there can be legitimate appeals to values of family, of community, of professional integrity, of constitutional rights and democratic norms, of courage, of the positive virtues in a given national or ethnic tradition. Such appeals can help give substance to the deeper loyalties of faith without becoming idolatrous.

I recall preaching one Sunday on the "gays in the military" dispute early in the Clinton administration. The issue before the country was whether homosexuality, per se, should be sufficient grounds for exclusion from the nation's military forces. A few days earlier, a high-ranking officer testified before Congress that he would not want to be responsible for his gay son's safety if he were in the military. The implication was that his son would be subject to harassment and harm from fellow soldiers—in other words, that military discipline could not be maintained. In dealing with that kind of argument, I strongly affirmed the importance of the American tradition of ultimate civilian sovereignty over the military and expressed my confidence that the enlisted personnel and officers of our armed forces are perfectly capable of obeying the law and honoring the chain of command. I was displaying more faith in the military values and virtues than the officer who had sworn to uphold them. It was a point I could make with integrity, for I believe it consistent with ultimate faith in God—even though one would not ever want to treat those democratic and military values as ultimate in themselves.

Principle Four:
Deal Responsibly with Objections

This book has emphasized throughout that prophetic preaching is not necessarily infallible preaching. While the freedom of the pulpit is to be respected, this does not mean that people are bound to agree with everything they hear. A preacher must not just *assume* agreement with his or her position on controversial questions, must not run roughshod over contrary views held in good faith by people who honestly do not agree. Bearing in mind that we ourselves might have taken quite a while to arrive at our present views, should we not allow others at least equal time? Often we will be surprised to discover that other people are not as slow as we were, but a measure of patience is still called for. In any event, we should not take up a controversial issue—knowing that some within the gathered congregation will be in disagreement—unless we are prepared to take time to deal with the objections responsibly. A former seminary teacher of mine used to say that in sermons we should not sideswipe the tough issues. By that, he meant we should not state our view more or less in passing, without explanation. To do so only inflames the question, making it more difficult, not easier, for people to change.

The sermon time is not normally a good time for open dialogue (though creative ways of doing this can be devised for exceptional occasions). But a preacher's good faith in dealing with objections can be both symbolized and given substance by scheduling dialogues or "talk-back" sessions later. Such sessions can give everybody an opportunity for further growth.

Principle Five:
Do Your Homework *before* Preaching

Some years ago, when I was on a college faculty, I received a telephone call on a Monday morning from a clergy acquaintance in a nearby city. He had dealt with a hot subject in his sermon the day before and had run into a firestorm of criticism from parishioners at the door when the service was over. He was calling to be sure that what he had said in the sermon was in fact true. I heard him out. Yes, I said, I believe your conclusions on that subject were right. But, I went on to say, as gently as I could, the time to do your homework is *before* preaching the sermon! The more controversial the subject, the more important the homework. Whether or not there is to be a talk-back session, one's preparation should be so thorough that one could deal responsibly with all sorts of further questions. That, at least, is the ideal. Practically speaking, we may not be able to anticipate every possible objection. But we should try. One way of trying is to get into conversation with people who are real experts on factual aspects of the subject and to do some preliminary talking with people whose views we know to be different from our own.

Principle Six: Deal with Part of an Issue If You Can't Deal with All of It

Some subjects are too large and complex to be handled responsibly and with the appropriate theological grounding in a single sermon. Then it may be helpful to have a series of sermons on the subject—though a whole series of sermons on a single social issue may not well serve the broader needs of a congregation. Alternatively, it may be possible to take up different aspects of the issue over a period of time in sermons not devoted exclusively to that issue.

I am more concerned about attempting to be definitive in treating a subject about which we do not have definitive knowledge. Global warming and genetic engineering are, for example, issue areas about which competent scientists disagree. The pulpit cannot hope to settle the empirical questions. We may still be able to say some things about what responsible Christians should do in the absence of definitive knowledge. Such preaching, necessary as it sometimes is, should be modest. It should be less "thus says the Lord" and more "this is the way it seems." Of course, some aspects of the question can be "thus says the Lord"! For instance, while aspects of international trade agreements are technical and in some cases experimental, the economic well-being of poor people everywhere, as God's children, belongs in the "thus says the Lord" category.

Principle Seven: Strike a Balance between Principle and Detail

We have already considered, in chapter 5, the importance of specificity in dealing with issues and problems. The gospel is not only vague and abstract; it is concrete and immediate. This translates homiletically into striking some kind of balance between generalization and application, between principle and detail. The principle suggests *why* something matters. The detail helps us see *that* it matters.

As I write this, the recent film *Amistad* has provided a very graphic—and accurate—portrayal of the brutalities of the slave trade. Seeing it drew me back to John Wesley's eighteenth-century essay "Thoughts upon Slavery," an equally graphic description of those same evils. Wesley's essay did not neglect principles, drawn from theological reflection on the liberating love of God, but the detail helped the reader see what that love of God should mean in respect to an awful practice. Wesley's views influenced and supported William Wilberforce's crusade against the slave trade. Largely because of that crusade, Parliament made the slave trade illegal, and the British navy acted on the high seas to impede it. The end of the slave trade, and ultimately of slavery itself, cannot be attributed solely to the writing and preaching of John Wesley. But it does illustrate the importance of helping people see, in some detail, the evils that contradict the deeper theological values and principles by which they live.

Principle Eight: Appeal to Our Common Stake in Justice

Justice can be understood as the institutional ordering of society in such a way that all are enabled to participate in their common humanity. Justice is not just something we claim for ourselves, nor is it simply our moral sense of the legitimate claims of others. It is a recognition, enforced through law and custom, that we all depend upon community. Justice is there for all of us. The pulpit can underscore the need to help people see that the rights of others are also our rights, so that our own experiences of injustice will make us more sensitive to injustices experienced by others.

There is a familiar quotation, attributed to Martin Niemöller, about his experience during the rise of Nazism. When they came for the Jews, he reported, he didn't speak out because he wasn't a Jew, and when they came for the Catholics he didn't speak out because he wasn't a Catholic. So when they came for him there was nobody left to speak out. Whether or not he said this—or in what form—the point is worth pondering sometimes in the pulpit. There is a good deal of self-interest at stake in our defense of the rights of others. The other side of the coin, especially applicable when preaching to a congregation predominantly made up of any of the world's disinherited people, is that there are other people who suffer injustice too. The community organizing techniques of the late Saul Alinsky famously emphasized the specific grievances of the people being organized. They would march on city hall (literally or figuratively) to demand change. Unfortunately, those who secure changes on that basis have then sometimes turned around and inflicted injustice upon others. But justice must be for everybody.

Principle Nine: Offer Hope

Prophetic preaching deals not only with problems and evils to be overcome; it offers hope that they *can* be overcome. This was the hallmark of most of the great biblical prophets, and it has been a striking contribution of the African American pulpit. No matter how wretched the situation may be, no matter how powerful the forces of evil that confront us, no matter how futile all aspirations may seem—still, nevertheless, it is God's world, so there is always hope.

Hope, to the Christian, comes in two dimensions. As eschatological hope, it is our expectation of God's ultimate victory over sin and death. It is the hope beyond history. Even though sin and death cannot be totally defeated in this life, in this world's history, God's creative purposes will eventually prevail. We can have confidence that in the end our trust in God will be sustained. That is the eschatological hope. At some points in history, that has been about all the hope available to beleaguered Christians. In some situations the almost exclusive emphasis upon eschatological hope has been prophetic, giving people the strength to continue to face their hardships with grace and courage.

But hope must also be within, and not only beyond, history: the eschatological hope, so to speak, invading the historical sphere. People cannot long sustain efforts in pursuit of goals they consider unattainable, no matter how desirable those goals might be. As a poem by Coleridge puts it, "Work without hope draws nectar in a sieve, and hope without an object cannot live." Even as a prophetic message about this world's ills is set in the ultimate eschatological framework, it must also offer hope that something can be done here and now. A good sense of history is helpful. How often in the past have evils appeared insurmountable, but somehow people of faith have managed to be the instruments of change. History never entirely repeats itself, but such lessons can rekindle hope among the discouraged. The late Raymond Wilson, longtime executive director of the Friends Committee on National Legislation, used to say that any important legislative reform requires twenty years of patient effort. My own experience as an observer of the Washington scene suggests that sometimes it takes longer than that, and sometimes not quite that long. The interesting thing is that, when the time is ripe, the change can come with lightning speed. It is possible for spiritually mature Christians to work hard and patiently if they have hope that in the end, somehow, their work will not have been wasted.

Principle Ten:
Suggest Responsibilities

A persistent question in the wake of a strong prophetic sermon is: Well then, what should we *do*? It is a fair question, but it can be a hard one to answer. I have sometimes heard it, after challenging a congregation with some issue or problem, and not had a ready answer. I suppose one should be ready with marching instructions; often they should be embedded in the sermon and not have to be solicited later. The reason why the question is sometimes not easily answered is that different kinds of actions are appropriate for different kinds of people. If it is a plea for action or reform at the political level, the general answer can be: Talk it up, vote intelligently, write your representatives in government, and otherwise use whatever political power you can muster. Even to gain a new sense of the importance of one's vote would be progress for many people. George Bernard Shaw once defined democracy as that system of government under which people get what they deserve. Unfortunately, there has to be a codicil: It is the system of government under which people have inflicted upon them what *other* people think they deserve. In any event, there are about as many specific answers to the question of what one should do about public policy as there are members of a congregation. We all have our unique points of access. Sometimes here, as elsewhere, those who hear the sermon may be better fitted to answer the question of their personal responsibility than the preacher.

Somehow, though, that is not enough of an answer. Unless *some* concrete suggestions are ventured, at least *some* of the time, the impression may be gained that our only response can be to moan and groan. A few suggestions, occasionally given, can release the flow of ideas within the whole community of faith.

Of course, some kinds of actions can well be undertaken by the congregation as a whole. A plea for greater community involvement in the prisons—long overdue in most parts of the country—can result in a church-sponsored prison mission. Concern over the needs of public schools can result in an education mission, offering tutoring assistance and morale-boosting support for teachers. Problems in city government can result in a mission group, some of whose members attend city council meetings, to become more knowledgeable about the issues and to locate the points at which other members of the congregation can be enlisted to help out. Sensitivity to homelessness can create motivation for sponsorship or co-sponsorship of shelters, soup kitchens, and free legal and medical service agencies. The pastor does not need to assume personal responsibility for all such things, but the pulpit can be a great motivator.

nine

Traps to Avoid

In preaching, as in any other form of communication, it is possible to undercut one's intended message unintentionally. Most of us commit fallacies of logic from time to time without quite realizing it. When we do, we weaken our credibility and our message—at least in the long run and certainly among thoughtful listeners. I wish in this chapter to note a few of the traps we can fall into inadvertently.

1. Inconsistent Appeals to Authority

All moral appeals are validated finally by some norm. Ultimately (I would contend) the authority is theological. But then there is the question: By what route has the theological norm been brought home to us, and how is it validated? The most tempting source of authority is the Bible, and with good reason. It is, sine qua non, the primary written basis of our faith. But how are we to use it? The Bible is full of teachings on a wide variety of issues. When a specific passage supports a point we wish to make (or when we derive the point we wish to make from our reflections upon a passage), we may simply use the passage as authority. The message becomes, in effect, This biblical teaching is true and binding upon us *because it is in the Bible*. But if we rely upon a particular proof text in this way, we are unconsciously committed to accept every other biblical passage on every other issue.

I have known both "conservative" and "liberal" preaching to fall into this trap. Some kinds of conservatives will be happy to identify all homosexuality as sin, on the basis of passages in Leviticus and Romans, while avoiding passages in Matthew on love of enemies or in 1 Corinthians on women keeping silent in church—or, for that matter, other passages in Leviticus prescribing the death penalty for homosexuality and assorted other infractions of what are taken to be divine commands. Some kinds of liberals will exactly reverse this order, while also making quite moralistic use of the parable of the last judgment in Matthew 25. Biblical literalists are quite willing to be fully consistent in uniformly appealing to all scripture as immediately binding. But then, upon closer examination, there is the problem of inconsistencies within the Bible itself.

We don't escape the problem by avoiding scripture, either. When some version of natural law is appealed to as norm, we may find some aspects of the natural created order more compatible with our predilections than others. The same is true of appeals to tradition, that vast sea of accumulated Christian experience on the selective basis of which almost anything can be justified as having rich Christian precedent. Even the attempt to escape the trap by appeal to nonobjective sources of authority, relying instead upon the inner guidance of the Holy Spirit, does not work. Have not numbers of Christians attested diametrically opposed divine commands based upon deep inner conviction?

The best way to avoid the trap is to be honest about our limitations. There definitely is a subjective factor; at the same time we are given deeper insight into the faith by serious biblical study, by attending to Christian tradition, and by taking the factual world seriously.

2. Generalizing from Single Cases

A single, emotionally compelling story can have enormous rhetorical impact in a sermon. Usually it will gain and hold attention and be more persuasive than statistical presentations and erudite quotations. But a single case can be an exception, and generalizations must be based upon a broad number of cases—not just one.

Still, there are two ways in which even a single story can be honest as well as helpful. First, it can be an illustration of a truth arrived at by a wider measure (such as accurate statistics or a broad personal survey). Second, it can serve as a way of countering a *wrong* generalization, providing at least some evidence that the conventional wisdom is wrong.

3. Treating Contraries as Necessarily Contradictory

Some things that appear to be opposed to each other are really more complementary than incompatible. Most of the great ideological debates feature such misplaced conflict. For instance, is human nature individual or social? Clearly, we are irreducibly *both* by nature. To choose one over the other is really to eliminate both. Should we be concerned about conserving human society or changing it? Again, the answer is we have to be concerned about both. There is much in human society that needs to be changed, but some kinds of changes should be resisted to the death. Is freedom our basic norm, or is social responsibility? Again, neither makes much sense without the other. It is a trap to emphasize one pole in a polarity over the other that is its necessary complement.

4. The "Straw Man" Trap

Even in sermons it is possible to misrepresent the views of others in order to attack them more successfully. But don't! It is more honest, and in the end more effective, to present the views of others in their strongest, not weakest, form. A good rule is to be able to state somebody else's views even more effectively than he or she can before noting where they fall short. Perhaps that rule should govern our comments on other religions, about which most preachers know so little anyhow. I will have to confess that my knowledge of Buddhism and Hinduism is very superficial; my acquaintance with Islam—though better—is still weak. I know the basis on which I would judge these faiths; it would have much to do with the extent to which they embody faith in the God whom I find revealed in Jesus Christ. But I would expect these faiths to have truths to share that would make a real contribution to my own. In any event, I would not judge them on the basis of their most objectionable beliefs or practices or on the basis of their most reprehensible followers—any more than I would want to have Christianity judged by its worst expressions.

5. Poisoning the Wells

The graphic name "poisoning the wells" is given to one of the classical fallacies in formal logic. The idea is that if you put poison in other people's wells and they drink the water it will kill them. By analogy, if you poison your adversaries' reputations, you will kill their ideas without having to refute them. That is the stock-in-trade of demagogues. In the 1950s, McCarthyites, by successfully labeling people as Communists or Communist sympathizers during periods of Cold War hysteria, were able to eliminate people whose *other* ideas they opposed. I'm not sure how much out-and-out character assassination occurs in the pulpits of the land—probably not much. But personal attacks on the character of people is a singularly poor way to proclaim a gospel of love.

6. The Non Sequitur

Using non sequiturs is another classical fallacy in logic; it means, in Latin, something that does not follow. It is when we state a conclusion on the basis of something that may have little or no connection. For example, I do not like okra, so it must be bad for my health. Or, it's Wednesday, so it must be raining in Paris. Non sequiturs appear frequently in public debate and not infrequently in sermons. One of my favorites is the line that there has been a great increase in juvenile crime, drug use, and other social ills because the Supreme Court declared formal prayer in public school classrooms to be unconstitutional; you'd have to deal with a whole lot more to be able to prove that point, including consideration of all the other variables involved in late-twentieth-century social pathologies. Or to say that since Christianity is known to foster kindness and personal self-discipline, the atheist Charles Brokerton must be mean-spirited and dissolute. Or, since Rosemary Schwab is an ardent feminist, she must be an inadequate wife and mother. Our cultural stereotypes are loaded with non sequiturs, as we attribute all kinds of motives and moral failings to people solely because of the category we have placed them in.

In their insecurities, Christians may be tempted to reach out for solutions to perceived cultural problems that are no solutions at all. Far from indulging in non-sequitur assertions, preachers should help people find more realistic ways of understanding and dealing with their problems.

7. The "Ritual Function"

For this trap I am indebted to sociologist Robert Merton,[19] who observed that when goals and values are considered impractical or unattainable (or in deep conflict with other goals and values to which we give higher priority), we will substitute social rituals and formalities for realistic efforts. We may think the abolition of poverty unattainable, but we can still order up yet another sociological study of the poor, while also providing food baskets for selected poor people at conveniently spaced intervals. Rituals help us feel good about ourselves. They help us preserve the illusion that we are still strongly committed to goals that have in fact largely been abandoned.

I'm not sure I like Merton's choice of terms, since "ritual" is a word closely associated with worship, and worship is the lifeblood of the church. Does worship itself help us substitute illusion for serious commitments to social good? I do not believe it necessarily does, as I discussed in chapter 4. Worship, in fact, can touch us in ways that deepen our commitments. But let us be honest: Worship can also play exactly the role of ritual function. It can spin an illusion about our values and commitments that is at odds with our existence and practices in the real world.

That is, in fact, one of the most subtle traps into which even prophetic preaching can fall! Our very proclamation of truth—in the teeth of evil and injustice, so to speak—can lead people to believe they have engaged in the struggle just by supporting our freedom to speak in this way and by listening to us preach. How do we avoid the trap? Certainly not by abandoning worship and preaching, or even the small-scale works of mercy a church can undertake. I think it is rather by making our worship all the more focused and our preaching all the more incisive. For the ultimate subtlety is how a social ritual can itself become leverage for greater engagement with the problems of the world.

8. The Naturalistic Fallacy

This idea I owe to G. E. Moore, the turn-of-the-century British philosopher.[20] Moore, in a critical response to nineteenth-century British Utilitarianism (a philosophy based ultimately on the pleasure principle), argued that we cannot identify a thing as being good just because it exists. Hence the fact that people are motivated by pleasure does not mean that pleasure is "good" or that efforts to increase our happiness are necessarily good either.

Moore's alternative is a bit convoluted and beside the point here, but the concept of the naturalistic fallacy is interesting. How often we identify the good with what people are known to want. Or, a more telling temptation for clergy, to identify the good with the numbers of people who are attracted to something or other. We forget that large numbers of people—even a large majority—can be very wrong. We must take great movements and widely held attitudes seriously, but not as final tests of truth. There is here a special word for a prophet's sometimes lonely vocation: Our calling may be to stand against the stream, working for a time when the stream's direction will change.

We could explore still more logical fallacies and traps about which we need to be wary. We will not always avoid them, try as we will. Sometimes we forget. Sometimes we are drawn off our spiritual center. Sometimes we just get tired and can't think as clearly as we wish we could. But it is always possible to return to that center of our selfhood and learn better how to preach that whole truth in love.

ten

Learning from Criticism

In a not-so-cheerful moment, the prophet Jeremiah reflected on the uneven rewards of his calling: "I have become a laughing-stock all day long; everyone mocks me. . . . [T]he word of the Lord has become for me a reproach and derision all day long. . . . All my close friends are watching for me to stumble" (Jer. 20:7–8, 10). He is tempted to give it all up but feels driven to continue. "If I say, 'I will not mention him [the Lord], or speak any more in his name,' then within me there is something like a burning fire shut up in my bones; I am weary with holding it in, and I cannot" (Jer. 20:9). The saying "No good deed goes unpunished" must have, as a corollary, "No prophetic word goes uncriticized!" In that respect, we can claim no special privilege that was denied to Jeremiah. As a consolation prize we may sometimes remember the words of Jesus: "Woe to you when all speak well of you," and take comfort that we have at least escaped that woe. In any event, we must not be surprised when opposition and criticisms come. Sooner or later they will.

When they do, we may be tempted, alternately, to succumb and give up before the opposition or to revel in a martyr's role. Both are spiritually dangerous and practically unproductive. To give up is to abandon our centeredness, our integrity as spiritual beings, while allowing the opposition to carry the day. To revel in the martyr's role is to substitute our own ego for the word of God we have been called to proclaim. Self-righteousness tends more to stiffen resistance than to lead others to change.

Of course, the truly exasperating thing about criticism is that the critics may be right! Or at least partly right. When they are, can we be big enough to learn from the criticism and to grow? There is a special grace to being willing to change, even to reverse course. This is never easy, but if our fundamental commitment is to God and not to our own ego, we must be willing to hear from God through the lips of our opponents.

We have already attended, briefly, to the intellectual problem of moral judgment—how to reach for moral truth. That discussion underscores the intellectual and moral handicaps under which we all operate: We are sinners and we are intellectually limited. We do not have all the truth, and we are not morally perfect. A certain humility is in order. I find that in Jeremiah. In addition to the soul-searching in chapter 20, Jeremiah sometimes retreated in the face of opposition, no longer as sure of his ground as he had been before. Then, having licked his wounds and reflected more deeply, he returned with much more confidence in his message. That can be our experience as well, although sometimes our confidence in what we have been saying may need to be shaken.

How can we respond to opposition and criticism in such a way that the truth we want to represent is expressed faithfully and effectively? I wish to suggest six main points.

1. *We can convey an openness to hear what others have to say,* although that doesn't mean retreating from the truth as we understand it until we are persuaded. The courtesy of listening can be extended to even the most outrageous viewpoints. In fact, the more outrageous they are, the more important it is that we really do hear them! Having listened, we can more legitimately claim the right to be heard ourselves. And having listened, we can respond more intelligibly.

2. *The fact of the conflict may lead us all to reach for deeper common ground.* Even the most intense conflicts can be at a fairly superficial level. Often we talk past one another because we are not struggling to understand the deeper ground where, in fact, we may be closer to those who disagree with us than either we or they suspect.

Several years ago I found myself subjected to a good deal of criticism from the evangelical-to-fundamentalist press. Some of the opposition was, I supposed, aimed less at helping me toward a closer walk with God than it was at warning suggestible Christians against the spiritual dangers of more liberal churches such as ours—with a more than passing implication that it would be a mistake to support any political leaders who regularly attended such churches. As a result of this publicity, I was invited to be a guest on several conservative Christian radio talk shows. I suspected the invitations were designed to polarize the radio audience even more with a direct exposure to error, which could then be criticized at the talk show hosts' leisure.

I accepted most such invitations, provided the shows would be live and unedited, in the hope we could find some common ground. I tried to subordinate my natural tendency to score debating points. We did sometimes disagree on inflammatory issues. But it was surprisingly easy to locate a deeper level of common ground in God's grace and our common humanity—and in the mutual recognition that we are all sinners and God is greater than any of us. Those are, after all, implicit in an authentically evangelical position. Many a preacher has discovered that what seems to be a polarized situation in a local church does not represent the deeper beliefs of supposed antagonists.

3. *Sometimes opposition and hostility have their source in psychological or social frustrations with little or nothing to do with the content of the sermons themselves.* I learned that lesson early in my ministry. In a church I served one summer in the Deep South during a period of maximum racial conflict, I was surprised to discover only one family I could fairly characterize as deeply racist. This family was also going through a variety of economic and health-related problems. As I came to know them better, it was pretty clear that the racism was more effect than cause. That didn't make it right, and the racism of such people can be just as dangerous as any other. But it does help us see that the healing has to come at a deeper level. The sad fact is that extremist movements have generally been fueled by demagogues manipulating the frustrations of marginalized people. It helps if we can see and respond to such realities and not take unfair criticism personally.

4. *We should try to say some kind things to the critics as persons.* We must never engage in demonizing others, and it is important to avoid any implication that the rejection of the *ideas* of others means we are rejecting *them*. One thing we can count on: What we say or write is almost certain to be repeated—and likely to be distorted.

5. *Remember that the most vocal critics may not constitute a very high percentage of the congregation.* The fact that people are more likely to make noise when angry or against something can lead to a distorted picture. The intensity of the opposition or criticism can mask its low numbers. The danger is that we may feel drawn into spending disproportionate time and energy in responding. Normally it is a mistake to take on one's critics in sermon form, and we should not be overly defensive even in less formal settings.

As a kind of metaphor for this, I am reminded of a scene in the vice presidential campaign of then Senator Hubert Humphrey. Speaking from the rear of a train to an audience of hundreds, he was distracted by four or five young hecklers who had managed to position themselves right in front of him. He was goaded into responding directly to their taunting questions. Most of the crowd couldn't hear what they were saying, only his answers. He was a superb campaigner, but in that moment he forgot a very basic point: He had the microphone and they did not! If he had continued addressing the crowd at large, ignoring the critics, they would have had very small impact. Sometimes, when critics are only a small and irresponsible minority, it is possible to carry on with the main themes of a preaching ministry while reaching out to the opposition in a more pastoral way.

6. *Departures are not necessarily bad.* No pastor should want to drive anybody out of the church. Our pastoral responsibility extends to everybody, and we need to cultivate the kind of community spirit within our congregations in which people can express their heartfelt differences without animosity. That said, people do sometimes move on when they become too uncomfortable with sermons. We grieve over that, but the integrity of a free and responsible pulpit is too precious to sacrifice when people threaten to leave. It is not all that uncommon for newcomers

to more than make up for the departures. Even if that is not the case, the spiritual growth and commitment of the remaining congregation may get a boost. A clergy friend told me of a small crisis he had to go through as a result of his preaching. A few people left, and he was disheartened. He expressed his discouragement to his bishop, a wise older man, who remarked with a smile that "sometimes we have to add by subtraction."

Nobody likes the subtraction. We would far prefer to have no opposition at all and, when there is criticism, for it to be constructive. But whenever it is said that a good pastor will always be able to get along with everybody, we must not allow ourselves to forget Jesus and the prophets. Jesus was not crucified because of his failure to be a good pastor! Jesus was not crucified because of his failure to love. He was crucified because he did love—and they didn't! His love led him to be very pointed about the personal and corporate sins that undermine God's intended realm of love and justice.

Having recorded these comments, I must, in honesty add a bit more. Criticism can be very *painful*. More than one pastor has pondered why, within a community of faith and love, there should be such infliction of pain. Of course, the church is not immune to sin—nor are those of us called to be pastors and preachers. Nothing about the pastoral office itself can spare us if we are not growing spiritually. Paul Tillich once remarked to some theology students that "the theologian must pray twice as much as anybody else." Perhaps, in view of the temptations and the stress that often accompany prophetic preaching, we should make that "three times as much as anybody else" for the preacher.

Responding to Criticism
from beyond the Church

Most of the criticism we receive is likely to be within the community of faith itself. The congregation is the primary audience and, truth to tell, the rest of the world is not likely to pay much attention. In fact, many a prophet is frustrated not by the criticism but by the inattention! Who *cares* what we say?

But that is not always so. When we deal with broader issues effectively, we may have to confront a whole new set of critics. Most of what I have already said about learning from criticism applies in the case of outside criticism. But there is this further problem: The broader public is not likely to know us and be able to put our words in context. Indeed, malicious critics may take delight in quoting us *out* of context—but that can happen unintentionally as well as by design. Our problem is that we may find it difficult to respond, even to retract our errors, in ways that reach those who have been influenced by the critics. I once had to endure the consequences of inaccuracies published by a critical columnist in three hundred newspapers, without any prospect of being able to respond in the same venues. Painful as that was at the time, I discovered that the public attention opened up other avenues of communication and that there was also a lot of support out there.

An immediate dilemma is whether to respond at all to criticism that seems unfair. If we do, we may simply give wider circulation to the charges. But if we do not, the criticisms may go unanswered—and be deemed by some to be unanswerable or accurate. On the whole, I think it better to respond if one can do it with a grace that does not indirectly diminish our message. Sometimes it is better to trust others to do the answering for us, so the issues are not allowed to become too personal. Of course, when we have been wrong, we need to acknowledge that and get on with life! And in any case, whether the criticisms have come from within or beyond one's own congregation, one must remain steadfastly conscious of the humanity of even the most severe and unfair critics. A gospel of love is meaningless if it does not include them.

In the hard times we are likely to find quiet encouragement from mature Christians of the congregation and from colleagues in ministry. We who share the high calling of pastoral ministry need to support one another in those moments of distress and to remind one another that we share something deeper even than our common calling: the love of God who is the source of the truth we proclaim.

PART II

SERMONS

Introduction

The following sermons were preached at Foundry United Methodist Church, Washington, D.C., from 1992 to 1998. I do not offer them as models of what prophetic preaching should be. In one way or another each represents my struggle to give voice to the gospel of love as it confronts us amid the dilemmas and confusions of contemporary life. We never know to what extent we succeed in that. We can be sure that we always fall short of the mark. I hope my own struggle, reflected in these sermons, will prove helpful to others. I preface each one with introductory comments about the specific setting and the problem or problems I sought to address.

I agree with a comment made by Dr. Martin Luther King, Jr., in the preface to a volume of his sermons. Dr. King noted that sermons are meant to be heard, not to be read. The spoken word and the written word have much in common, but they are not precisely the same. In speech, the cadence of voice, gestures, facial expression, and eye contact contribute greatly to the communication. On the one hand, it is not always necessary to complete sentences—but on the other hand it is necessary sometimes to *repeat* sentences to be sure they have been heard. Written style is different enough that a simple transcription of what was actually said in a sermon can be less effective than a carefully crafted essay on the same subject. Still, there is a spontaneity in the spoken word that I believe can and should be preserved in published sermons.

I generally write a full text of a sermon, then re-outline it several times, partly to improve it and partly to fix it more easily in the short-term memory bank. In delivering the sermon, I speak without manuscript or notes, except for an occasional quotation I wish to read with precision.

The sermons that follow were transcribed from tape recordings of the sermons as delivered. I have made some editorial refinements to improve the smoothness of reading, but I have sought to keep such changes to the minimum.

Truth Heals

On September 20, 1992, I faced one of the most difficult situations any preacher can confront. That week, my predecessor had sent a letter to each member of the congregation acknowledging that he had crossed boundaries "of a sexual nature" with parishioners. He had retired only two and a half months earlier, after a very effective ministry of twenty-seven years. That ministry had been enormously important in the lives of many people and had helped develop the historic Foundry Church as an inclusive, caring congregation. His ministry had included an influential television program reaching far beyond the church.

The letter came as disillusionment to many and threatened to polarize the church between critics and supporters. I clearly had to set aside previous sermon plans and address this situation directly. In the course of an administrative board meeting that had been called earlier in the week to discuss the crisis, a member remarked, "Remember, only the truth heals." As I pondered the next Sunday's sermon, that comment kept coming back to me. What was "truth" in this situation? Truth for those who had been hurt? Truth for those who had been helped by a long ministry? Truth for the church as a community of faith?

The text from John was, I thought, exactly right.
(Readings: John 14:1–10; 8:31–32)

I do not often, or lightly, change a sermon topic that has been announced in advance, or the scripture going with it. This has appeared to be one of those weeks when I should do so. The new sermon topic was suggested to me by a remark made by one of the members of the Administrative Board last Monday night. In the midst of our discussion, as many points of view and feelings were being expressed, she said, "Remember, only the truth heals."

Only the truth heals. That brought to mind a part of the scripture today: "you will know the truth, and the truth will make you free." I found myself asking, "Could that really be: The truth heals? The truth makes you free? Are there not truths that hurt? Cruel truths? Hard truths? What could it mean that the truth heals?" Searching for an answer, we first turn to our other scripture in John, which raises the question, "What is truth?"

What is truth? I have to confess, I am not thoroughly pleased with some of the words John chose. Perhaps I'm offended that John did not consult me! I freely acknowledge that none of my writings have been canonized. So we shall have to make do with John's: "I am the way, and the truth, and the life. No one comes to the Father except through me. If you know me, you will know my Father also. From now on you do know him and have seen him. . . . If you continue in my word, you are truly my disciples; and you will know the truth, and the truth will make you free."

Let's bracket off questions having to do with whether non-Christians can be saved (which I strongly believe) and issues of theological language, and proceed to the heart of the matter. What is truth to John? Truth to John is Jesus Christ as revealer of God. In John we read those words, "And the Word became flesh and lived among us . . . full of grace and truth." In Jesus Christ we see what God is up to. We see what God is like. And all that we might say about grace infusing human life, and defining us, and gathering us—all of that is implied in these words. God is truth. Not just *a* truth!

> God, the very center and source of all being,
>   in whom we live and move and have our
>   being.

God, who has given us the gift of life.

God, who in Christ has given us the gift of
grace.

God is truth to us. Now that raises the question, How shall
we deal with the relationship between truth and fact? We
often use the words interchangeably. It will be said often in
conversation, "Don't confuse me with the facts. I already
have my mind made up." We wonder whether that means
somebody doesn't want to look at reality. That is not what
John means, but there is implied here a very important distinction between truth and facts. Indeed, journalists know
that well. A journalist is called to the high task of separat-
ing out those facts that are decisive in interpreting the truth
from those that are not, bearing in mind the interpretation
we bring to the factual world is what is decisive in our understanding of truth about the world.

The journalist Wes Pippert has this to say about the distinction between truth and fact in his excellent book *An
Ethics of News:*

> Objectivity is often held up as a journalistic ideal, but em-
> phasis on objectivity can obscure truth at times. Objectivity
> may become the mere presentation of two sides of an issue
> in a way that distorts the proportionate importance of each
> (p. 5). . . . Truth is not to be confused with mere accuracy.
> Even accurate facts can mislead or deceive (p. 7). . . . [T]ruth
> contains the core, the essence, the nub, the heart of the mat-
> ter (p. 11).[1]

To John, the truth containing the core, the essence, the
nub, the heart of the matter is God as revealed in Jesus
Christ. I've just finished writing a history of Christian
ethics. I'm not a historian. For me this was exciting, a venture into bringing together history and Christian ethics. If I
ever had any doubt about the importance of the selectivity
of facts, I do not now. Out of that vast canvas of human
history and Christian reflection upon it, I—humble servant

that I am—had to decide what the reader will consider to be important truth. An awesome responsibility! Truth is not just fact. Fact can obscure truth. Truth is the interpretation of fact. In Jesus Christ we have the clue to interpret truth. Sometimes we seek to evade truth, because we do not have a sufficient grasp of the source of the truth. Look at it in a very personal, humorous way: Every morning when we get up and look in the mirror, we see facts that may not be entirely to our choosing, and we may seek to rearrange the facts more thoughtfully. We are all like this. Every human being is like this. There is nothing wrong with that. Just don't mistake the rearrangement for ultimate truth.

I wonder now about the situation we are confronting in our church. You may wonder how much to share, and with whom. We've adopted a feeling here at the church that we are an open church, a receptive church, all are welcomed. We do not hide anything. We are decent. We understand that the truth is deeper than the facts, and we summon people to see the deeper perspective. But in a situation like this, you may wonder how to speak to your friends, or children, or others. I cannot answer that question for you. I can say that here, as in a family, it is probably a mistake to be deeply concerned yourself and yet to withhold what that concern means from those who are close to you, bearing in mind that the way things are shared must always be age appropriate, to be helpful to people at the time and place of their need. I am not a professional psychiatrist, nor do I intend to be an amateur one, but I think there is psychological reason to be open, to let the healing start from the ground, from the bottom.

Organizations like Alcoholics Anonymous have helped us to understand the importance of that. You know how the ritual goes in Alcoholics Anonymous meetings: "I am so-and-so; I am an alcoholic"—that from somebody who perhaps has not touched a drop for years! It recognizes that alcoholism is a part of the reality of that person's life, and he or she stands in need of help from others who also are alcoholic. The company of people in Alcoholics Anonymous understands that the outpouring of God's grace can be enormously helpful at the point of their facing the reality. Is that not true for all of us? We have to touch the bottom, and then we can understand that the God of grace has been there before we have, and God will lift us and help us grow together.

What, then, are we to say about what has happened in our midst in the church? If the truth heals, and if it is God's truth that heals, what are we to say? Clearly, the first truth is the truth about each one of us, that we are God's children. I don't know about you, but I find myself reflecting sometimes, "What are the facts about my life that I would *not* want anybody to use, to define me?" In my case, I can think of one or two—hundred. On the other hand, what are the facts about my life that I would like to have define me? I can think of one or two—period. But the fact that does define us is that we belong to God. That is the fact. We belong to the God who knows all the other facts, and who is there to help us, in grace. What freedom, what healing there is in knowing that God already knows it all, and that we go to God who is the source of our grace. Truth number one.

The second truth has to do with the feelings and attitudes we bring to this situation. Your staff here at the church has been very busy this week, talking with many people in the congregation. I suppose I have personally talked with two or three hundred, either individually or in small groups, all over our parish. I've heard from so many in the parish; they mirror my own feelings. And, indeed, the conflicting feelings run through each of us. It is not very good advice to tell you to suppress those feelings. But remember the Arab proverb: "A friend is one to whom one may pour out all the contents of one's heart, chaff and grain together, knowing that the gentlest of hands will take it, and hold all that is good, and with the breath of kindness blow the rest away." I find myself thinking again, in the words of the old hymn, "What a friend we have in Jesus." God is our friend. God is like that.

Don't suppress the feelings. You can't go around them. You have to go through them. One of the problems with abuses in counseling relationships is that they may make it more difficult for people to face their feelings honestly, understand them, and grow through them.

Therefore, a third truth has to do with the damage, the harm, the hurt. Bearing in mind that everybody is hurt in situations of this kind, we think of our former pastor and his family. What an avalanche of prayer has gone up from this church, this week and now, for them! It may be a bit harder to think of the women who are involved. They too need an avalanche of prayer and understanding. We're learning a lot more about how these situations develop in the lives of people, the harm that can be done, and what may be needed to heal. We know that in our society women—children and men too, although probably mostly women—have suffered silently. We have to resolve, as a culture, as a whole society, that this *must* stop, so that the hurt doesn't continue silently. We think of all the people in the church who're hurt. The truth is *there*. The truth is that there is hurt there.

The fourth truth has to do with a ministry of the past twenty-seven years. This truth is that very great good has come to large numbers of people. It is God's good, working through human channels to help us all. Do not say no to that. Do not submerge that. That is true. That is a part of God's truth.

I want to confess to you that when first I stood in this pulpit and enjoyed the enormous privilege of preaching to this great congregation, I knew a lot about what you now know. It had been shared prior to the agreements between all the parties, with an understanding of confidentiality. At the time it was not known whether the information would become public, and I carried the weight of that, as did a very small number of others in the congregation. I want you to know that when I spoke on that occasion about the history of this church, and specifically about the history of the last twenty-seven years in this church, everything I said then I would say again now, including the joy of the retirement celebration you had together in June.

Do not feel you need to rewrite history. You can never rewrite history; that history is in your soul. The only way you can rewrite history is to say no to a part of yourself. That is part of the truth. I also want to mention the truth of the integrity of the leadership of this church. I have marveled, in these months we have now been together, at the quality of that leadership. I do not mean just the ability to lead. I mean the ability to lead with integrity, compassion, and Christian depth. And what do I mean by the leadership of this church? Not some elite. I mean all of the people of this church, because everybody here is a leader in some aspect of life, in our life together. I want to reaffirm my confidence in the leadership of this church.

Now the final truth that comes to me this morning, as we lift our eyes above the horizon of this sadness and these events in our midst, is that we see how God is brooding over this church and is setting us in mission. God has a very important agenda for this church. Here we are, situated at one of the great intersections of modern life, in the heart of a great city, in the heart of the nation's capital, with a voice to the world, to the nation, to our community, to ourselves. God has high hopes for this church, great dreams for this church. Together as we work as Christians in mission we will experience those hopes, those dreams, those missions. One of the wonderful things about the history of this church, in at least the last decade and probably long before, is its great diversity. What that diversity means is that people of all kinds are welcome here and feel welcome here. Because of that we can be in mission to a world in which many people do *not* feel welcome, a world of injustice and tragedy and hopelessness. The word to us from God this morning is that we have work to do together in this church.

And what is the last word? Well, the last word doesn't

come from human beings. But the last word of this sermon will be from the Gospel of Luke, a word which comes to all of us together: "Do not be afraid, little flock, for it is God's good pleasure to give you the kingdom."

Out of the Miry Bog

Each year, on the weekend nearest Martin Luther King's birthday, the church gives special attention to the legacy of the great civil rights leader and the continuing problems of intergroup relations. In preparing to preach on these themes on January 17, 1993, I was intrigued by the words of Psalm 40, "He drew me up from the desolate pit, out of the miry bog." That, I thought, is the perfect metaphor for the continuing morass we find ourselves in regarding relationships with others.
(Readings: Psalm 40:1–4; Isaiah 49:5–7; John 1:29–33)

You've just heard these words from Psalm 40:

I waited patiently for the Lord. He inclined to me and heard my cry. He drew me up from the desolate pit, out of the miry bog, and set my feet upon a rock, making my steps secure. He put a new song in my mouth, a song of praise to our God.

"He drew me up from the desolate pit, out of the miry bog." The point is clear. Here we are in a swamp, and we can't extricate ourselves. We're in quicksand, and the more we try to get out, the deeper we go. This is a good symbol or metaphor of the religious life. The more we try to save ourselves, the more difficult it turns out to be. Paul would have understood that point very well. "Woe is me, how can I be saved?" he wrote. Here I am, he is saying in effect. The more I try to save myself by being good and by doing good, the deeper I get into the swamp.

And why? Because the more I try to save myself, the more preoccupied I am with myself, the more self-centered I am. Self-centeredness is exactly 180 degrees away from the life of love in which we find our salvation, and yet one cannot seize the life of love. Unless one has been seized from outside one cannot enter it. Paul would have understood that psalm very well.

I think Psalm 40 may have some important things to say to us this weekend, when we celebrate the birthday of Martin Luther King and the impact that he and the civil rights movement have had on the United States and the world. There is a certain risk in even raising the issue, and I want to acknowledge that risk right up front. It is that if we become too self-conscious about it, we can also sink back farther into the miry bog. Some months ago, one of the members of our congregation who is African remarked to me that at the time of the Rodney King incident in Los Angeles, with the civil disturbance, the miscarriage of justice, and the heightening of tension in this country, he found that everywhere he went, he was conscious of this polarization, this conflict—until he came in the door of this church, and then he could forget it. Now that is a tribute to this church and at the same time a description of where we want our country to be. Not self-conscious, but affirming our common life together and putting aside all of those old polarizations, all of those old conflicts.

But in order to get to that place as a society, it pays to take account of the history of where we have been. Not to know that story, not to repeat that story so that we learn from it, can be a serious mistake as we try to take hold of the future that has been offered to us. We easily forget just how deep the swamp was in our society before the civil rights movement came along. It had as its tragic roots, of course, the history of slavery, hundreds of years in which persons were dehumanized and oppressed, many perishing long before their time. And those who survived, living in shackles without the dignity of their own humanity conferred in their so-

cial conscience. The tragedy of slavery. And no sooner was
that over when, after the brief period of reconstruction following the Civil War, the shackles of Jim Crow came into
place and our society became segregated and our culture
profoundly influenced by racism, discrimination, racial prejudice. That is our history.

What did that history mean? Martin Luther King stated it
with great eloquence on many occasions, probably never
better than in his celebrated "Letter from Birmingham City
Jail." Do you remember the background of that letter? He
had been chided by religious leaders, including if I may say
so a couple of Methodist bishops, for pursuing his agenda
too quickly. It was important to be more patient, they said,
and he shouldn't be using these militant, aggressive means.
Well, here is his reply. "I guess it is easy for those who have
never felt the stinging darts of segregation to say, 'Wait.'"
King continued with a litany of the evils African Americans
had had to face—the lynch mobs, the "hate-filled police-
men," the "airtight cage of poverty." Most poignantly, he
described the feelings of inferiority suffered by his little
daughter upon being told she couldn't go to the amusement
park she had just seen on television—and the pain of having to tell her. And how hard it was to respond to a little
boy's question, "Daddy, why do white people treat colored
people so mean?" Perhaps white critics could think again
about why it would be so hard to wait.

Meanwhile, of course, all of these effects on African
American people had their reciprocal effects in the white
community. The culture had become profoundly corrupted
by racism. We forget sometimes that the first victim of oppression can be the oppressor. The German philosopher
Hegel understood that clearly as he spoke in the first part of
the nineteenth century about the effect of slavery. "If you
enslave another person, what you are doing is depersonaliz-
ing, not only that other person but also yourself. Because
you have cut off the possibility of genuine human interaction, you have devalued the response that you might get

from the slave and your own humanity cannot be affirmed."
To put it differently, if you think of the issue as a matter of
skin color, if you depersonalize another person because of
their skin color, then you have announced to yourself that
the only thing important about you is your *own* skin color;
there is nothing in you deeper than that. *That* is dehuman-
izing. And of course, in retrospect, we know that such profound dishonesties infected our whole culture.

Let me cite one example from my own experience back
in the 1960s, which by now is ancient history to many people in this room. Still, it's an important memory, in the immediate context of the civil rights movement. I was living
in California at the time and was asked by Pacific Gas and
Electric Company, the big public utility company of northern California, to serve as a consultant on business ethics.
Once a month, for a two-day period, I would meet with different strata of management in that big public utility to talk
with them about their dilemmas in business ethics. This was
part of a regular two-day package of meetings, most of
which were led by the company leaders themselves. I was
always invited to dinner the evening of the first day.

Much to my shock, when I attended one of those din-
ners, where I was only one of two outsiders present, the
manager of one of the many divisions of the company stood
up and, slightly inebriated, began talking about the difficulties of observing and enforcing the Fair Employment Practices Act, which had been adopted by California. He used
language I cannot repeat in a family pulpit to characterize the
people he was concerned about. The bottom line was he
didn't want to hire anybody from a particular minority
group. So far, he said, he had been successful in putting this
off. But, he said, "One of these days somebody's going to
come up just when we're hiring and will be a graduate of
the University of California and we'll have to hire them and
then, first thing you know, because of that education we'll
have to promote them. And then they'll be bossing white
people." Now this was said with a certain public relations fi-

nesse in the presence of an outsider, but you can imagine
the feelings of the top company officials from San Francisco.
One who was in the room cast furtive looks in my direction.
And, you can also imagine the discomfort the next morning
as we talked about business ethics.

My point today is that out of public sight the grim reality of racism was played out. But I found the deepest dis-
honesty voiced by the person who was trying to smooth
everything over. He said, "You have the wrong idea. In the
other divisions of the company, they know that if you hire
one or two, then the FEPC will let you alone." Now that's
the kind of corruption of spirit we're talking about, infect-
ing all aspects of American society, north, south, east, and
west. We were in a miry bog, and we could not get out.

Indeed, the Supreme Court school desegregation decision of 1954 had helped to show the way and had, in fact,
mapped some progress. But by the beginning of the 1960s,
the momentum established by that great decision had begun
to plateau. And in the words of a book published in that period, so far as the South was concerned, the Deep South said
"Never." Now one might say that the civil rights movement
came along in a timely way. Martin Luther King's bus boy-
cott in Montgomery, Alabama, occurred in 1955. In 1960,
the sit-in movement in Greensboro, North Carolina, helped
to open up the whole movement, which spread among students in ever-growing concentric circles until this became
the moment of possibility in American history.

The civil rights movement was important for two reasons.
First, because it was the vehicle by which African Americans
were able to assert their own dignity and insist on being
treated fairly and in the same way as others in our society.
History teaches that with one voice an oppressed people finally must take responsibility for its own freedom. Why? Because it is very easy for an oppressing group to dehumanize
those who are not asserting their humanity. That responsibility, of course, posed enormous dilemmas for people in
the black community in our country, who had every reason

to fear serious reprisals and further difficulties. But that was a moment of truth and a moment of courage among people in the civil rights movement. They were able to act militantly, resistantly, even aggressively in the assertion of their rights.

Second, the civil rights movement was deeply dedicated to reconciliation. The agenda was desegregation and integration—that is, the inclusion of African American people in our society along with all others. And using methods of nonviolence affirmed even the oppressor and thereby extended a hand to help the oppressor out of the miry bog. This was a marvelous moment in American history. It was the moment of real possibility for our whole society to move out of its miry bog.

Was it a religious moment? Some might say that it was not really religious, but rather a secular movement; indeed, that it took its inspiration from Gandhi in India, who was a Hindu, and that it used secular methods and oughtn't to be understood as a particularly Christian thing. Well, just to set the record straight, Gandhi credited his insights in this area to Leo Tolstoy, the great Russian thinker who was devoted to nonviolence as a form of resisting evil. And, to complete the story, Tolstoy got his major ideas from Adin Ballou, a great New England clergyman who had begun to use and write about nonviolent methods in the struggle against slavery. Things come full circle. I don't know if any of that really matters. What really matters is that God reached down through the civil rights movement, whatever its origins, to speak a word of persistent love and to say that our society cannot have peace except on the basis of justice and love.

I want to share two other stories from my own engagement with the civil rights movement that illustrate to me in different ways how profoundly spiritual it was and what its impact was upon our society. One of them is from Selma, Alabama, and the great campaign to establish voting rights that gripped this country in 1965. At the time of the Selma march, people flooded into town from all over the country to participate in this movement together. I was one of them, a young professor from California. I shall never forget the spiritual impact of this thing. The combination of prayer meetings and strategy sessions and rallies and worship and communion engaged every facet of our existence in that moment. I don't think I have ever experienced anything quite so gripping in its integrity.

I remember one moment in the midst of the campaign when a couple of busloads of young people arrived from San Francisco. They were going to be super militant and they were going to take over. They were all white college kids, I think, and they moved into town, into Selma, and they were going to show everybody how it was supposed to be done. They didn't have any patience with this religion stuff. They went to the meetings because that was where planning occurred, but they did not enter into any of the prayers. For a time, they threatened to upset the equilibrium, the balance, of the movement, until one old black man stood up in Brown's Chapel AME Church where the efforts were centered and pointed his fingers at these kids and he said, "I don't know why you're here. We can't keep you from being here, but as far as we're concerned, if you're not here because of God and because of love, you don't belong." And that sobered the occasion and illustrated for us all the deep spiritual basis of the civil rights movement.

The other story is a story on myself. After Martin Luther King was assassinated in 1968, this city—Washington—was aflame. Some of you will remember the great clouds of smoke rising; 14th Street was in ruins, the 7th Street corridor, H Street. Many of us were trying to help out as best we could, bringing food in, doing other kinds of things. That was over Friday, Saturday, and Sunday. On Monday, a memorial march was scheduled to be held in memory of Martin Luther King in Memphis, Tennessee. I was delegated to represent Wesley Seminary as a part of that demonstration. By the time I got to Memphis, I was completely burned out, completely on edge, in total tension, deeply concerned that the coming march would help to heal, to reconcile, and yet fearful that it would not. We got off the plane and were immediately taken to the area where the march formed with thousands of people. Each of us was given a sign with a slogan: I AM A MAN, which was taken from the garbage collectors' movement there, or WE SHALL OVERCOME, or another slogan from the movement.

Just a few days earlier, Martin Luther King himself had been involved in a march like this in Memphis, but it had been taken over at one point by some who didn't understand and respect the movement, and it had disintegrated in chaos. As I stood there waiting for the march to begin, I was deeply afraid that somehow it would not take the right turn. And then, ahead of me, two or three rows, I saw a young black man, probably early college age, beginning to write his own message on the blank side of his sign. I thought, Ah-ha, here we go, somebody is going to take it on himself to put his own message out and distort the message of Martin Luther King and this movement. Looking over his shoulder, I saw him form the letters *I H A*. And by free association, for which I express no pride, what flipped into my mind was the thought, This is going to say I HATE WHITEY. And he turned his back a little way and continued to write, and then I could see again what he was writing and it said, I HAVE A. This time what flipped into my head by free association, for which I again express no pride, was I HAVE A GUN. That is what I thought! He continued to write, and then he hoisted his sign, and you know what it said? It said I HAVE A DREAM! Now, that young man was God's word to me in the lineup to the march, reaching down to me to say, Don't be afraid of this movement. This movement intends good for our society. This movement intends to bring us together in this society. This movement belongs to God.

And so, as we pause, we ask ourselves, are we out of the bog yet? Well, no. At least not all the way out. There are a lot of encouraging signs in our society. Don't be afraid to affirm those encouraging signs. Don't be afraid that that will cut the nerve of further action by making us complacent. We're not going to be complacent. But take strength from what God has already done through that movement and through the millions of people who have been gripped by it and who have begun to transform our society. Already it is clear that that movement has done irreparable good! And as we take stock of our future, we might well remember the words of another old black man in Selma. The night before the march was scheduled to go to Montgomery, he stood before that crowd in Brown's Chapel AME Church and looked at the children there. Remember that these children had been thrust into jail and been mistreated and had still sung the songs of freedom and of love and had helped to energize that community for a great historic role in the transformation of American society. He looked at these children and he said, "The things you have done here are the stories that mothers will tell their children for a thousand years."

I do not know if that is so. I do know that the things those children did there, and the things the civil rights movement did in our society and continues to do through people like you and me and others in this community, belong to God and therefore belong to all eternity. And all that we do in helping to further extricate our society from the miry bog is for the ages.

The Heavenly Vision
and Our City

This sermon, preached on February 7, 1993, was the second in a short series of sermons on the general theme "The City of God and Our City." Here I reflected on the biblical vision exemplified in Revelation 21 and its relevance to contemporary urban life. While the sermon was addressed principally to a Washington, D.C., congregation, it dealt with pathologies and possibilities characteristic of other cities in this nation and around the world.
(Readings: Psalm 48; Revelation 21:1–7, 22–26)

This is the second in a three-part series of sermons dealing with the City of God and our city. Last Sunday, we explored some of the painful realities of the city. Today, we want to look at the question, Is there a Christian vision for the city? Is there a heavenly vision for the city? A good place to begin is that text from the book of Revelation. You recall again the words:

> I saw a new heaven and a new earth; for the first heaven and the first earth had passed away. And the sea was no more. And I saw the holy city, the new Jerusalem, coming down out of heaven from God, prepared as a bride adorned for her husband.

"I saw the holy city, the new Jerusalem, coming down out of heaven from God." Now that is a part of the Apocalypse of John of Patmos, which deals with faith in quite colorful imagery. It is not to be taken in literal detail but in the spirit of the proclamation of the triumph of God. Of course, the Apocalypse was written during a time of persecution, when Christians were suffering at the hands of the Roman Empire. And so the imagery of the Roman Empire, the beast, and Christ doing battle with the beast is very colorful and powerful. In the midst of this is the marvelous portrait of a new Jerusalem, the city of God.

This may not be immediately applicable to Washington, D.C., but I think there are two rather interesting observations we can make of that portrait of the new Jerusalem. The first one is that John is using urban imagery. It is city language. This is not the bucolic meadows and fields or forests; there are no cows mooing in the distance. This is a city, this is urban. The idea of a city is that people dwell rather closely together and interact. The portrait of the interaction here is a very positive one: People get along well in the new Jerusalem as portrayed by John of Patmos. In this city where people dwell together, the streets are of gold and the gates are of pearl.

You might ask, is this city of God, although a city, also a rather intimate place of beauty and interaction? Well, not really. Because, if you want to read part of the passage that was not read as part of the scripture today, you will note the dimensions of the holy city: "The city lies foursquare, its length the same as its width; and he [the angel] measured the city with his rod." Fifteen hundred miles wide, fifteen hundred miles long, and, to make the point additionally, fifteen hundred miles high! By my rough calculation, that would be roughly the same size as the United States of America east of the Mississippi River, not even counting the suburbs. Rapid transit in that kind of city would mean the Concorde going from one end to the other! This is a big, big city. Possibly John of Patmos had at least Los Angeles in mind, I don't know. I'm trying to underscore that this is a *city* he is talking about. Now, that is not to say that God has no intentions or concerns about the rural areas, too. But, this imagery in Revelation is urban. It's about a city.

Second, it's not simply a city in the by-and-by. Often the hymns we sing about the new Jerusalem carry the message that this is a reality you experience after you die, and no doubt that is a legitimate way in which to use the imagery. But notice! He is speaking about the new Jerusalem "coming down out of heaven," for, as he continues, "the dwelling place of God is with humanity." So we have a link between heaven and earth through the holy city. And thus we can ask the question quite legitimately: What is it about the heavenly city that can be translated into the transformation, the change, of the earthly city? That is our question today.

Too often, when we think of Christian faith, it is in such radically personal and such exclusively "spiritual" terms that we omit the reality that through and through the Bible is concerned about the enactment of the life of the spirit in the world. Indeed, speaking of cities, you might sometime want to look up the entry for "city" in a complete Bible concordance. You will find many hundreds of references to cities in both Old and New Testaments. City is a pervasive reality. The question is, Can a city be transformed in accordance with a divine vision?

Augustine wrestled with these questions in his great work *The City of God,* written over a period of years following the first "great catastrophe" suffered by the city of Rome. The eternal city, master of the known world, was successfully attacked in A.D. 410 by barbarians who came sweeping in under the leadership of Alaric. They totally trashed Rome, pillaged the place, and three days later departed to leave a Rome that could never be the same again. The myth of the eternal city had been punctured. The question of this great earthly city was now before its people: Could Rome survive what had happened? Augustine, the dominant mind of the church, then serving as bishop of Hippo in North Africa, was challenged: Is it not because Rome is now Christian that it has become weak, now that it has substituted the soft virtues of love and caring, faith and trust, for the courageous, stern virtues of the old Rome?

Augustine wrote *The City of God* in response to that question. His answer was no! Rome's destruction was built into the constitution of Rome from the beginning. Rome was built upon self-love, but the city of God is built on the love of God. And so he contrasted this imagery of the city of earth and the city of God. The city of earth, he said, is made up of all those who love themselves even to the point of being contemptuous of God. The city of God is made up of those who love God, even to the point of being contemptuous of themselves or their own self-interest. Well, what about the endurance of Rome through all of those centuries? Augustine pays high tribute to Rome, noting the nobility of its leaders. But he also shrewdly observes that Rome, through it all, was still based upon self-love because of the love of its leaders for honor and recognition. And these, in the long run, were disintegrative virtues. Love of self leads to disintegration. Love of God leads people to draw together.

Isn't that interesting imagery when applied to the modern city—including, especially, this city that we love? We ask ourselves, Where are the resources of mind and spirit that lead to deep public-spiritedness, that lead to the subordination of self-interest to the good of the whole? That is the question that an Augustine would ask, in light of all of the harsh realities we have to confront. But when we look at our beloved Washington, D.C., and ask ourselves, Can there be a vision for the city? we may need to be reminded that without a vision we will always remain in the quagmire of the hard realities.

Francis MacNutt, who has written many books on healing, makes the interesting point that "healing begins in the visualization of health"—that is, in seeing yourself healthy as the starting point. Now, that doesn't mean you won't die. It doesn't mean all illness can be cured. It does mean that health is impossible without a visualization of health. He applies this, of course, to individual human beings. I want to apply it to the city. For us to be a healthy city is to see what health means in a city like Washington.

We begin, of course, with some very positive things, for Washington is not all downside. What a beautiful city Washington, D.C., is, with its lovely parks and broad vistas, its noble monuments! (I think we must have a monument in this city for every horse that ever lived!) What it can be like in the springtime, with the azaleas and the dogwoods and the cherry blossoms, when there is magic in the air in our community! Sliding over the slight embarrassment of summertime, what could be better than the fall, with its beautiful colors? Actually, every season is gorgeous; this is a beautiful, beautiful city.

And it is a city with marvelous civic facilities. Think of the libraries. If you're interested in a book, almost any book that has ever been written, if it still exists somewhere, you're likely to find it here in Washington—sometimes through interlibrary loan or, if you're really patient, in the Library of Congress, the greatest library on earth. Indeed, not to make too fine a point of it, the greatest library in the history of humanity is in our city. Or think of the museums along the Mall. What city on earth has anything quite like that? A total education available to you if you'll spend the time to wander through the Smithsonian and its different exhibits. It's completely free to the people who live here and visit here. Or the concert halls and theaters, the marketplaces and restaurants, bringing resources and styles of cuisine from all parts of the earth. What a well-furnished city Washington is!

And what do we yet need? We can only name some of the things that the heavenly vision might mean for our city. Certainly it would mean public safety. That is basic to the well-being of all cities. We must be able to walk the streets by day or night without fear. We must be able to visit in the parks, to spend time in the evening and experience the wonders of nature brought into the city in the parks. I think of Meridian Park, up the street from here a mile or so: a marvelously beautiful spot. I don't advocate going there at dusk and enjoying the breeze, though, because it's not really safe at this point. In a heavenly city, Meridian Park would be a perfectly safe place, as once it was. The same is true of Rock Creek Park and the other parks in this city. The streets and parks and highways and byways of the city need to be safe.

I am constrained to add that at a time when the Virginia legislature is considering very important measures regarding more gun control, this legislation could help rid *our* streets of guns. A very important component of the heavenly city is getting rid of all of those guns. I mean no offense to our neighbors two blocks away, the National Rifle Association, and I am sure that hunting and target shooting and things of that sort can be accommodated legitimately, but the enormous firepower present in our city streets is beyond control as long as weapons can be gotten on the other side of the Potomac River. I pray earnestly that the Virginia legislature will act wisely today and this week and at least help us begin to edge away from the reality of guns in our streets.

We think of the homeless on the streets and in the metro stations. At my own neighborhood station the number of homeless persons sleeping out is up to seven now, all neatly lined up. One sees throngs of homeless people on the streets of this city, begging, sleeping in places of some security. Many are in crude shelters; some of the official shelters are frightening places for the homeless and they choose not to sleep there. I do not know what the final answer is. I know the complexity of the reasons people are homeless. But I think I also know that in the city of God, nobody has to sleep out there, on the sidewalks by the metro station in sub-freezing temperatures—or at any temperature. With the marvelous architecture and the many buildings in this city, can we not put our minds to sheltering people who are poor and homeless and do it rationally and carefully and compassionately? Is that beyond our resources of mind and spirit and budget as a city?

Surely in the city of God, people can find a place to dwell and a place to work. Our unemployment rate is too high. Everybody in the city of God should have the opportunity to make their contribution and achieve a reasonable livelihood. That would be a part of the meaning of the heavenly city. And what about our children? Does not everybody in the heavenly city have the right to begin life whole and healthy? Some accidents of birth are preventable; the deplorable infant mortality rate of this city is preventable. Only about 43 percent of the infants here are inoculated by age two! There should not be a matter of chance in any government program; each should be universally guaranteed for every child in this city.

We have in this congregation a delightful person who is a public health nurse, one of those who actually visits homes. But she personally must serve an area of the city with a population of 150,000. Even so, she tells interesting stories about what a difference her ministry of nursing makes in the lives of young and old. Can we not extend that kind of service to broader ranges of our population as we reflect as a nation upon health care delivery? We need to think of what that means in our beloved Washington, D.C.

Think about education. Given the crisis in our city regarding young lives, and the grave difficulty of teaching children who come out of deprived homes often infected with drugs and other pathologies, surely in the schools of a community like Washington there should be a very high number of teachers in proportion to students. That is the secret of the success of the private schools—a lot of personal attention. Should that not be the reality for all children? Attention and achievement should not depend on whether you have the money or happen to qualify for some program targeted to a particular population. Education in the heavenly city is universally available to all children.

We can speak on and on about the pathologies of our city and what can be done about them. I think the heart of it, really, is our vision. It is our ability to lay other things aside in order to confront the enormous challenges facing us as a community. It is to say that we are a public community, and we are going to be public-spirited citizens because God cares about the city and all the people who dwell within it.

Walter Rauschenbusch, the turn-of-the-century Baptist theologian known for his leadership in the social gospel movement, was also a great mystic and poet. His *Prayers of the Social Awakening* are some of the most poignant expressions of a mystic spirit of prayer-centered life in all of Christian literature. Hear these words from his "Prayer for the City":

> Oh, God, we pray for this the City of our love and pride. We rejoice in her spacious beauty and her busy ways of commerce. And in her blessed home where heart joins heart for rest and love, help us to make our city the greater home of our people, where all may live their lives in comfort, unafraid, living their lives in peace and rounding out their years in strength. Grant us a vision of our city, fair as she might be. A city of justice where none shall prey on others. A city of plenty where vice and poverty shall cease to be factors. A city of brotherhood where all success shall be founded on service, and honor shall be given to nobleness alone. A city of peace where order shall not rest on force, but on the love of all for the city, the great mother of the common life and wheel. Hear thou, O Lord, the silent prayers of all our hearts as we each pledge our time and strength and thoughts to speed the day of her coming beauty and righteousness.[2]

The Motherhood of God

I chose, on Mother's Day, May 9, 1993, to speak on the earthly damage done when exclusively male metaphors are used to characterize God. Such language permits the assumption or conclusion that somehow men are more like God than women are. I was a bit amused when newspaper accounts of the sermon the following day spoke of the sermon as being about "how God can be a woman." Of course, the point of the sermon was that, although God is personal, God is not to be identified as either gender. But perhaps I also needed to remember how easy it is to be misunderstood. Deuteronomy 32:10–13 and 1 Peter 2:1–3 were the scripture readings for the day.
(Readings: Deuteronomy 32:10–13; 1 Peter 2:1–3)

How shall we name God? By what name shall we know God? For the ancient Hebrews, that was a very difficult question. God the ineffable majesty; God the power in whose destiny, in whose life, we find our destiny; God who controls the circumstances of human existence. How shall we name God? The one whom we approach in prayer. How shall we name God? The Hebrews were afraid to say "God is this," and to use a name directly, even the word we pronounce Yahweh. In fact, we're only guessing at how it should be pronounced because there is no tradition of how to pronounce the divine name.

You know the story of Moses at the burning bush. Moses receives a communication from God to go to Egypt and let his people go. Finally, after Moses is persuaded that, indeed, there is no escape for him but he must go to Egypt, he asks God, "Whom shall I say sent me?" And then we have that enigmatic answer, "I AM WHO I AM, say I AM has sent you." Now, without getting into a treatise on grammar, that is a rather interesting answer, isn't it? God is not the object of the sentence, God is the subject, "I AM." You will not put God in a pigeonhole, Moses; you will not say God is a thing alongside other things. "I AM WHO I AM."

Now, the Old Testament has a variety of descriptive words for God: king, shepherd, rock, father, even, at certain points, fortress, soldier, warrior, commander. These words are understood to be pointers toward God; they are not the name of God. And, indeed, one can see why that might be. Would you want to call God "rock"? You could say God in some respects is *like* a rock. But immediately you think of ways in which God is *not* like a rock: God is eternal; rocks last a long time. God is strong; rocks, relatively speaking, are pretty sturdy. Rocks cannot think or feel or have compassion, but God can. So in some respects, God is like a rock; in other respects, God is not. And similarly, all of the other words for God in the Old Testament work, up to a point, in suggesting the character, the life, the nature of God. But God is more than any single descriptive term.

Great Christian theologians, from the first, understood that point. Take Clement of Alexandria, for example. Clement had a very keen sense of how God is more than our words. Listen to this:

> If we name God, we do not do so properly. Terming God either the "one" or the "good," or "mind" or "absolute being," or "father," or "God" or "creator" or "Lord," we speak not as supplying God's name, but for want we use good names, in order that the mind may have these as points of support so as not to err in other respects. For each one by itself does not express God, but all together are indicative of the power of the omnipotent.

Great theologians have understood that all the language we use is to point us toward God. God is always more.

Jesus uses different terms for God The parables of Jesus speak of God as a householder, or master, or mistress, as a widow who is looking for a coin, a king (indeed the images of God as king and the kingdom of God appear about a hundred times in the Gospels). Most of the time, we think of God as father, as expressed by Jesus. But, there is a very important message that goes with that term. When Jesus speaks of God as father, he uses the word "Abba," meaning something like Daddy, or Papa, a term of deep intimacy and familiarity, suggesting that God really cares like a good papa, a good daddy. And Paul says, "When we cry Abba! Father! it is that very Spirit bearing witness with our spirit that we are children of God." Now, Jesus did not mean that God is in every respect like a human father, certainly not biologically. God is not a biological being, God is no object, God remains the subject. God is "I AM." This is a pointer toward God that uses the language of familiarity in the family. God is Abba. That is suggestive. That is on the right track. In prayer, that leads us into intimacy with God.

There is, unfortunately, a problem that goes with using the word "father" exclusively for God, and only fairly recently have Christians begun to be sensitive to what that problem is. If God is exclusively father, only male, then God may love women, but in no respect is God like women. That is to say, if God is exclusively father, men have a point of identity with God that women don't have. I do not think this is only a little semantic quibble. Rather, it gets at the point of centuries of Christians treating women as second-class persons. If one's status is grounded in the very character of God, the identification with God as father logically confers a kind of status on men that is not given to women.

One might suppose that the use of "father" was never intended to be exclusive in that way. And yet, the long centuries of Christian tradition point again and again to women's being relegated to second-class status. Even now, a majority of the Christians on earth belong to denominations or churches where women are not able to be clergy. In the case of the United Methodist Church, only since 1956—very recently—have women been ordained as clergy. Some might say, "Well, why? Is it lurking in our understanding of what God is really like that we should treat half of the human race as ineligible to participate fully in the leadership of the church?"

I was pleased to note, in an article in *The Washington Post* this week, that some denominations are moving on this point, and the United Methodist Church has more ordained women now than any other denomination. That is less an object of pride, however, than a point of distress to think that there are still so many Christians who deprive themselves of the leadership of women because of a theological hang-up about the character of God.

The worst instance of this that I know of occurred at a small seminary I once visited. In that little seminary, which was quite fundamentalist in character, they did allow women to be students. But they could be students only if they would pledge in writing that their service would be as Christian educators, not as pastors, and that they would not serve as educators for men over the age of eighteen, and that this statement would be countersigned by their husbands or fathers. I'm relieved that we can laugh about this now, but throughout most of Christian history this would not have been a joke; it would have been the reality. My point is that this behavior is grounded in our understanding of God. By what name do we identify the divine?

I am sure that the issue of semantics is going to continue in the life of the church for a long time. We struggle with hymns. To what extent should hymns be altered? How should we deal with the psalter? I was a delegate to the 1988 General Conference that produced the hymnal we're now using, and I can still remember some of the compromises made over psalter and language questions. I think those language questions will continue to vex us for some years. And there is nothing wrong with that, if we work these issues through. I do want to make one simple point, however: There is nothing wrong with the use of the word "father" for God, but, equally, there is nothing wrong with the use of the word "mother."

Some people object to the use of the word "mother." But how can you speak of God as a rock but not as a mother— on Mother's Day, of all times? Yes, God is like a rock. Yes, God is also like a mother. Listen to Clement again: "In his ineffable essence God is father; in his compassion to us, he became mother. The father by loving became mother." Now, as a man, and as a father, I'm not sure I want to identify only with the ineffable essence and leave to women the compassion! Clement understands that it is possible to speak of God with language drawn from any good aspect of human experience. When we speak of God as mother or use feminine imagery for God, there is nothing wrong with that. In fact, to the contrary, it draws into our perception of God other good aspects of human experience and says God isn't just *this,* but God is down *that* road as well. This is a pointer to the being of God.

The scripture texts today, both of them, use feminine imagery. For example, "Like newborn infants, long for the pure, spiritual milk, so that by it you may grow into salvation—if indeed you have tasted that the Lord is good." This quote from 1 Peter uses the imagery of a baby receiving the milk of the mother, as receiving of the divine life. Or this one, from Deuteronomy, from which the beautiful gradual was sung today: "As an eagle stirreth up her nest, fluttereth over her young, spreadeth abroad her wings, taketh them, beareth them on her wings, so the Lord alone did lead him Israel, and there was no strange God with him." Now, without dousing you in biblical technicalities, this is an interesting point. I just read that from the King James Version. In the Revised Standard Version, the "she" and the "her" are replaced with "it." And in point of fact, the Hebrew sustains the use of neuter or neutral or masculine imagery, but it is interesting that the function described—caring, nurturing—is feminine. That suggests that the writer of Deuteronomy had a bit of a dilemma: How can you linguistically convey the imagery of a mother's caring with language that gives no option but the masculine gender?

So here we are, seeking to understand God, knowing that the clues we have drawn out of human experience are all we have. But those things that point us toward God as compassionate and caring, these we can seize upon and use.

Now what about those people for whom the terms "mother" and "father" are wrapped up in trauma and hurt? I suspect there are people in this congregation who have difficulty when thinking of either mother or father. I have known people for whom there was a good deal of hurt associated with one or the other of their parents, and in a sense God was the transcending of that pain, the recognition that even though one's earthly father was hurtful, God is what one didn't have as an earthly parent. I see that similarly with the mothers.

Certainly as we address God in prayer we want to use language for God that is helpful and conveys to us a sense that we are accepted by God, who really cares for us. Don't trouble yourself using symbols or images for God that you haven't quite come to terms with yet. There are a lot of good words for God that can be used. But, today it is Mother's Day, and we celebrate in a very special way the idea that the term "God as Mother" is a good one to use. God is like a good mother. I had a good mother and a good father, so it is a lot easier for me than it might be for some. And yet I know there are lots of good mothers and lots of good fathers, and we draw strength and insight out of the good mothers and the good fathers, helping us a little bit to understand the character of God.

We really have been speaking of how we understand God. In God, there is grounded the feminine side of existence as well as the masculine. The mothering as well as the fathering is all grounded in the character of God, as all good things are grounded in God's character.

There is another question, which goes a little bit further and may give us insight into how God experiences us. Does God experience us as father and as mother? Does our experience give us clues about God's experience? I thought of that in a special way this week when I received a letter from a mother. The letter told about her experience with feeding her infant and what a deeply spiritual experience it was for her. It drew her into certain kinds of insights she had never had before. In the letter, she refers to a writing by Simone Bloom, which said, "I often feel a spiritual communion with all the other mothers who are feeding their babies in the still of the night. Having a baby makes me feel a general closeness with humanity." And then this mother wrote, "I have come to feel a communion with God while breast-feeding my baby. A flowing of love and grace through me to the baby through the nurture and providing of love and comfort at the same time as nutrition and antibodies." In other words, she is saying she came to a deeper understanding of what God experiences through her own experience. I cannot verify that, for I'm neither a mother nor God. But isn't there a sense in which in the community of faith we are sharing our experiences of God and our human experiences? And the fact that this mother wrote me that letter has contributed to my insight, my understanding of the character of God. Even though I have not breast-fed a baby, nor ever will, this gives me a deeper understanding of God, just as all the experiences of good that we share together in the community of faith contribute to our deeper understanding of God.

On this Mother's Day, we think especially of that imagery; we think of the Motherhood of God, a symbol pointing toward very important aspects of God's being. We celebrate other kinds of experiences that people who are not mothers share with one another and with all of us, and out of it all we may not come to the point where we can attach a name to God, because we do not turn God into an object. But out of it all, we grow as a community of faith in our understanding of what God is like and what God's character is in God's dealing with us.

Matching the Mountains

During the summer of 1993, my wife and I accompanied a group of high school youth from our church on a work project in an Appalachian mountain community. We spent the week helping less privileged people repair and renovate their modest homes. The young people, having worked their hearts out, were in church on August 8, the day after their return. The service was designed in part as a recognition of their efforts. My sermon had several goals. It was intended to reinforce their sense of fulfillment in their accomplishment and their resolve to live a life of active service. And it was intended to challenge everybody in the congregation to understand the spiritual life in very active terms. The texts of the day were from Joshua 14 and James 1, two very activist passages.
(Readings: Joshua 14:6–12; James 1:2–4, 22–25)

Above the entrance to one of the state government buildings in Sacramento, there are inscribed these words, BRING ME MEN TO MATCH MY MOUNTAINS. Those words are taken from an early poem by Sam Foss, which goes something like this: "Bring me men to match my mountains, / bring me men to match my plains, / men with empires in their purpose / and new eras in their brains." Now, I will not nominate that for the Nobel prize in literature, and I think that both Sam Foss and the State of California need to learn something about inclusive language—remembering that women as well as men are involved in "matching mountains." But, having said that, the words are a rather interesting challenge, particularly in the context of the forging of the West, the creation, almost, of a new civilization in California. And while noting that all human history has its dark side, not least of all the creation of civilization in California, the achievement of people who matched the mountains proved to be quite stupendous.

"Bring us people to match our mountains." Isn't there almost a double meaning there? Think of things to be dealt with as mountains to be conquered, but think also how people who match the mountains become rather like mountains— with "mountain" as a metaphor for character—becoming sturdy and rugged and enduring.

"Bring us people to match our mountains." The themes of both the Old and New Testament lessons are caught up here. The Caleb story in Joshua is very interesting. Caleb, at age eighty-five, volunteered to take the hardest terrain in Israel. When the Promised Land was being divided up and other tribes wanted the low-lying ground where there was no great difficulty in settlement, Caleb volunteered to match the mountains.

Similarly, the New Testament lesson in James reads, "My brothers and sisters, whenever you face trials of any kind, consider it nothing but joy, because you know that the testing of your faith produces endurance. And let endurance have its full effect, so that you may be mature and complete, lacking in nothing." Now, you may not feel that all the trials you face are nothing but joy, as James has put it. And yet James is observing that what we *do* in an active sense has a lot to do with what we *become*. Our doing is also a becoming. We act, we deal with problems, and it affects our character. It affects what we become. "Bring us sturdy people to match our mountains."

I think of that in terms of people I've known or known about who have had overwhelming personal problems to deal with, some of them physical. For instance, a United Church of Christ minister I knew some years ago was born with no arms. And yet he learned as a child how to dress himself and how to get around. He went to school and completed graduate education, becoming in time a minister and a lecturer. I shall never forget the day he lectured in one of my ethics classes at Wesley Seminary and the time came to turn the page. I think the students were sort of wondering, How is this going to happen? He has no arms! Well, his foot was in a specially designed glovelike sock. When it came time, up came the foot and turned the page. A marvelous illustration of somebody who has learned to cope with what for most of us would be a truly mountainous kind of problem.

Or I think of another man I didn't know at all. Victim of a polio epidemic some years ago, he was on one of those hospital rocking beds that was used to help the person breathe. Looking at him in the hospital ward, I assumed he was asleep. His eyes were closed, his face was expressionless. And then I saw, alongside his body, his hand forming into a fist and then relaxing, forming into a fist and relaxing, and then raising slightly and then falling. And I realized I was watching a human drama—someone struggling to regain control of his physical body. I have no idea what finally happened to him. My guess is he came along. Whether he found complete restoration of his physical body, I don't know. But certainly he did much better as a result of this kind of effort.

I think also of people who confront emotional problems, and that is true now and again for all of us. The fears, the anxieties, the depression, the sense of low self-esteem against which many people struggle, sometimes throughout their lives. It doesn't help at all when you have what to other people are irrational fears and somebody says, "Well, you shouldn't be afraid of that!" Well, I am! Or, "Buck up, you shouldn't have that low sense of self-esteem. Don't be so anxious." That kind of word from people outside yourself is their way of saying, I'm superior to you because I don't have that fear, or that sense of low self-esteem, or anxiety. It doesn't help much to hear others say that, does it? But still, for all of us as we confront those nagging internal problems, it helps to try to match that mountain one small step at a time, knowing that every little bit one does to get on top is further liberation into our full humanity.

I suppose with the students here I should comment that it makes a big difference whether you choose the easy or the tough courses when you're in school. And whether you're addressing those problems that may appear mountainous in your life in school. Matching the mountains means taking on the tough problems. I find myself also thinking, this summer, of that drama we all witnessed on television night after night in the Middle West, the absolute catastrophe of the worst flooding there in all recorded history. With people working frantically hour after hour, day after day, filling sandbags, building extra levies, topping off the levies, and all too often, after many, many hours of backbreaking work, seeing the river crest a little higher and sweep it all away. I'm impressed by what I have seen in the human vignettes that have appeared on television. I suspect, long after the waters have receded and people have forgotten the personal damage they had to confront, many are going to look back upon this and say it was their finest hour. This was the time they really exemplified what it means to be human and to be a people together working to solve their problems.

But the message that I read in those words across the government building and in the scripture is not really limited to dealing with the problems you can't avoid. It's a question of going out and *seeking* the difficult challenges. That really was Caleb, seeking what he could just as well have avoided. Nobody is forcing a person to take on issues of homelessness or injustice in the world. There are many ways of avoiding the hard problems, but those who seek them out are the ones who carry the course of history on their backs. I am prompted this morning to say, concerning political leadership, It's easy to drift along in the political arena; lots of people do it. But to seek those issues that really are going to matter even though one must pay a difficult, hard, political price to deal with them— that is where history is always made.

And then, of course, I think of our young people again. You should have seen those kids! (To the young people: You can stop listening now!). I marvel. One of the things I learned is that there really is a difference between youth and age, I mean there *really* is! I saw these kids working away, dealing with the tar, carrying roofing up ladders, pounding away, putting up drywall, laying bathroom floors, and at the end of a hard day's work they'd be just totally exhausted in the van back to the center, just completely out of it. And then off to supper and a shower, and then they'd be playing basketball in the evening! I couldn't believe it! And I thought, These kids didn't have to come to Appalachia. There is a lot of hurt, a lot of suffering, a lot of need in Appalachia. We went to Harlan County, one of the poorest counties in the United States. More than a third of the people of Harlan County are below the poverty line. There's high unemployment, and what employment there is is in coal mining, a basically sick industry. There's lots of social disorganization and many evidences of physical poverty. It would have been easy to have avoided that task. And at a time when so many young people, and older people, are tempted to be couch potatoes, to see our young people going down there and pouring their hearts into this work—I found that very impressive. You can be proud of the young people of this church and of your own contributions to make that effort possible.

We can avoid the tough problems. But history is borne on the backs of those who do not. We learned a few things in a week in Harlan County. It's a county that figures in U.S. labor history in some interesting ways. There were some very bloody confrontations in the development of a labor union that sought justice for coal miners, a lot of heartache and tragedy. One of our youth groups had to confront a family that was almost totally disorganized, and we had to struggle with what it meant to be helping that family with its physical needs in the face of such disorganization. We found ourselves struggling to think about more than the task of putting roofing on a roof and paint on a wall. How do you really come to terms with the whole community, the whole fabric of humanity that is involved here? There are no easy answers, but what answers there are go with those who are willing to match the mountains.

What happens if you don't? I would like to be able to threaten something dire. I have a problem here, because I don't really believe in hell, so we can't threaten that. I would also like to be able to say that you'll be terribly discontent all your days. And yet I have seen people who took the easy way throughout life and were not particularly unhappy. I think what's at stake here is something a little deeper. It has to do with our basic humanity. The point is raised in an interesting novel by Frederick Buechner, *The Book of Bebb*. In this novel, the Rev. Leo Bebb is portrayed as a kind of jack-leg evangelist, seen alternately as a saint and a charlatan. But Bebb has saved the life of a man named Brownie. In the novel Brownie is very obsequious, always seeking to please others but without any real vitality in his life. We learn, as the story progresses, that Bebb literally saved Brownie's life in an act of faith healing, when Brownie had been clinically dead and Bebb brought him back. So Brownie has been saved by Bebb, but he still hasn't quite learned what it means to live. Bebb says to Brownie, "You've got to get in there and sweat and rub till your arms ache so the light can come through." And then he turns to another character named Antonio and says, about Brownie, "Now you take a man like Brownie, Antonio, and you ask yourself where the Almighty went wrong. Well, I tell you, it's not the Almighty went wrong, it's Brownie went wrong. The Almighty gave Brownie life, and Brownie never lived it."

That's the point. To be given that incredible gift of life, which has come to each of us in varying forms with varying histories, varying physical gifts, mental gifts, and social environments and backgrounds, for all of us, what an incredible gift is the gift of life! Can we live it? To be given the gift of life and never to live it, what a tragedy. To live it is to be engaged with life, to be involved. At the time of our death, maybe all of our past sweeps before our eyes, and maybe it doesn't. That probably doesn't matter. The real question is, Have we really lived? So that the gift we present to God as we conclude our life on this earth is a gift of love and caring and involvement.

There is a hymn by Maltbie D. Babcock that we used to sing a good deal more than we do these days. I've discovered with some regret that it's not in the new United Methodist Hymnal. Theologically, I suppose I can see why it might not be. But still it speaks to us.

> Be strong! We are not here to play, to dream, to drift.
> We have hard work to do and loads to lift.
> Shun not the struggle: face it, 'tis God's gift.
> Be strong. Be strong.

There is a sense in which we are here to dream. And, certainly life must also include play. But life is also struggle.

> Be strong! Say not the days are evil—
> Who's to blame? And fold the hands and acquiesce—
> Oh, shame! Stand up, speak out, and bravely, in God's name.
> Be strong. Be strong.

The struggle of life is God's gift to us. May God bless you in your personal struggles, those individual little mountains that each person faces. May God bless you in addressing those. May God bless all of us as we struggle as a community, as a church, as a nation, as a world in those vast mountains that loom before us. Let us match ourselves against the mountains.

The Street of People
and the Street of Power

Early each fall, Foundry Church recognizes and commissions the hundreds of people who serve through the various mission groups. Most of these groups are engaged in hands-on service of one kind or another, such as soup kitchens, housing for the homeless, AIDS programs, and similar community service. These are useful missions; indeed, it is necessary that such programs be provided by many churches in contemporary cities.

I wanted to help people become more sensitive to the connection between the needs we encounter on the streets and the power structures that affect their lives, sometimes causing the street problems. This sermon, preached on October 3, 1993, was suggested to me as I pondered the intersection at which the church is located—P and 16th Streets. P Street, largely residential, stretches through several demographic zones of the city. Sixteenth Street stretches north, from the church to the Maryland suburbs, and south, about one mile, to Lafayette Park and the White House. It struck me one day, as I gazed out my office window on the intersection of these streets, that one of the streets is predominantly about people, the other about power. In preparation for the sermon I walked a mile or two each way on each of the streets, carefully observing what I saw, entering buildings, talking with people. In the sermon I reflected on the highlights of what I had learned. I sought to draw the people part and the power part together, helping the congregation see how the power affects the people.

(Readings: Proverbs 31:8–9; Zechariah 8:3–6, 12–17; 1 John 3:11–18)

143

Little children, let us love, not in
word or speech, but in truth and action.
(1 John 3:18)

What do love and truth and action mean to Christians, gathered in this place, at this church, at the intersection of P Street and 16th Street in the heart of the nation's capital? If you will permit a little bit of sermonic license this morning, I want to take that intersection itself, located right outside, as a symbol or metaphor for the mission of the church, fully understanding that our church makes connection with more streets than 16th or P Street, and that people come here from throughout the metropolitan region and as visitors from around the nation and the world, and that the impact of power is felt on more than 16th Street. But if you will permit a little license, I want to take you on a walk along P Street and then 16th Street. And I will repeat for you experiences I had on a walk along P Street last Tuesday and on 16th Street last Wednesday.

I took the natural boundaries of P Street for these purposes to be Rock Creek Park. We'll exclude Georgetown from this, and we'll begin with Rock Creek Park at 22nd Street, and follow along P Street through Dupont Circle to 16th Street, a distance of about a mile, then on to North Capitol Street, a distance of an additional mile and a half. I saw many things and many people that day. One of the highlights was a horn honking at the other end of P Street and a member of Foundry Church waving her hand to me. I thought that was a good omen!

What did I see? I saw upscale apartment buildings at the other end of P Street; I saw a very fine hotel with a liveried doorman out front, waving in the luxury automobiles as they came and went; I saw a limousine passing by; I also saw a cluster of homeless men gathered close to an outdoor restroom facility, and the thought occurred to me, Yes, that's a rather natural place to gather if you're homeless, on the street. Two of the homeless, I noticed, were sharing a single cigarette. I saw a couple of young men in the window of the Burger King. One had an earring in his ear. I saw another young man riding along the sidewalk on his bicycle, bare to the waist. It was a warm day last Tuesday, and his arms, both arms, were covered with tattoos. And I thought, Perhaps there's a statement here, but I wasn't able to get close enough to read the fine print.

Continuing on, I saw the usual scene at Dupont Circle: dozens of people gathered in the park, immense human diversity, a very peaceful place, some homeless people lying on benches or on the ground, clusters of men gathered around the concrete boards. Indeed, the only evidence of conflict I discovered in Dupont Circle was the heated chess games at six or eight of these outdoor boards. And there was a group of well-dressed men with one woman, who appeared to be refugees from one of the neighborhood think tanks.

I proceeded on up P Street, past the elite Washington Club, and the Iraqi embassy, a flow of people up and down the sidewalk—rich, poor, black, white, gay, straight, couples, singles—an immense diversity of people, as we see in those blocks of P Street. I passed the Stead Recreation Park, which is right behind the church, heard the happy voices of children playing on the new playground equipment, and saw children in the new ball fields, directly behind the church, and in one-on-one basketball games at a skill level that I find awesome. I waved at Foundry Church.

I crossed 16th Street diagonally by the Carnegie Institution. There was a woman who asked if I had a dime to complete her little collection of coins so she could ride the bus. I don't know if she was homeless; I would guess she was. I gave her a quarter and went on my way, quite self-righteously.

I passed a barbershop that could have been a barbershop

on a main street of any town in the country, though it was ethnically specific. Across P Street, a couple of Asian employees of Duron Paint Company were instructing each other in a language I will never decipher. I continued up P Street past Logan Circle, a little bit like Dupont Circle, except here was General Logan with his sword drawn, on his horse, and I crossed P Street up to 11th Street. At 11th the street was blocked because there had been a storm the night before, and a tree had fallen and crushed an automobile. I asked whose car this was. Somebody told me, "A woman who lives in one of the apartment buildings," and I wondered about her insurance and how one deals with a sudden catastrophe that comes literally out of the blue.

I continued to 7th Street. There was a recreation park with clusters of men, and young children playing on the playground equipment. I would guess that perhaps a number of these men, if not all of them, were unemployed. It was during working hours on a regular day. I continued to 3rd Street. Between 3rd and 1st Streets is the Armstrong Adult Education Center, a beehive of activity, mostly concerned with helping people gain job skills and their general equivalency diplomas. An arrest was in process in front of the Armstrong Center. Police had handcuffed a young man and were bundling him into a patrol car. Then I saw a helicopter coming overhead, sweeping the neighborhood rather low, and up ahead, a block or so, at the corner of North Capitol Street and P Street, there were a couple of police cars with their police lights spinning. I talked with a student at the Adult Education Center and asked him what was going on, and he said there'd been a shooting at the elementary school, Cooke Elementary School. I continued on my way, but first I paused and asked the policeman if it was safe for me to continue, and he said, "Oh, sure, there's police up there." I continued intrepidly on up the block, and as I approached the scene, the police cars left. There were several people in tight little clusters, talking about what had happened. I don't know if anybody was killed. I suspect not, because in the next day's paper I found no reference to it, but an ambulance had come and taken somebody away from a building right next to the elementary school. There were no happy sounds of children coming from the school.

I crossed the street, and at the intersection of Capitol and P Streets there was a man who turned out to be an Iranian rug merchant, at a little carpet place. We got to talking about what had happened, and he said, "This happens all the time here, there are shootings all the time." He said, "These kids don't have any religion. That's their problem." He told me his door had been shot several times and he'd had to replace it, and even now the metal pull-down door—like a garage door—over the warehouse part of his shop, had bullet holes in it. I left him, and as I walked back this way I looked, and there were seven bullet holes in his door.

I continued back to 4th Street. Fourth Street scared me. There were all the stereotypical impressions of an outdoor drug market at work there. I proceeded quickly through that intersection. There was a billboard above it with an 800 hot-line for runaway teenagers, and I wondered how many run-away teenagers had used the number from that particular location.

At 3rd Street there's a Mom and Pop store. I went in and bought a little packet of crackers so I could talk to the pro-prietor. The thing I found striking about this little store—otherwise it was like any little store you'd find anywhere in America—was that the money, the cash register, was in an enclosed glassed-in cage at one end of the store. I went in and paid for my crackers and asked the proprietor, "What is it like here?" and she said, "There's shooting all the time. Just now there was a shooting up the block." She was refer-ring to what I had seen. "And yesterday some kids took shots at a policeman, the other direction, just within that block." I said, "How can you still stay here?" And she said, "I have no choice. This is our livelihood." I went out, and at that point, friends, I almost cried. As I reflected upon the chil-dren in the streets, the guns, the drugs, the life of the school, the families, I almost cried. And there across the street, another arrest was in progress.

I headed back up P Street toward Foundry Church, passing Shiloh Baptist Church, one of the great churches of the city, much engaged with missions of all sorts, paused to say hello to some of the people in Shiloh, noted there were two or three other churches along the street, and then I was back to Foundry, reflecting with fresh eyes upon the immensity of our mission to the city. We only scratch the surface of the depth of human wretchedness and fear in our work, and I think of God brooding over P Street, celebrating the wonderful diversity of its people and yet crying over what is happening to so many of those people. Clearly the mission of the church is to be engaged in a caring way on the street.

The next day it was time to walk down 16th Street from the church toward Pennsylvania Avenue, almost exactly one mile from our door to the front door of the White House. What does one see on the street of power? Immediately in the first block on 16th Street you pass the National Wildlife Federation. In the ecology field it has become one of the heavy players. It's a concentration of environmental concern groups, assisting with the passage of legislation and working to arouse the consciousness of America to the importance of environmental questions. I had a pleasant talk with some of the people; they shared their literature and spoke about their programs.

Then the Australian embassy on one side of the street and the Nigerian embassy on the other, and just across Massachusetts Avenue, and up a few doors, the Philippine embassy, and, if you strain your eyes, not too far away the bright blue and red flag of the embassy of Russia, these symbolizing how power plugs into Washington from all over the world—these four embassies, possibly others along the street that I'm not aware of, symbolizing the international character, an interlocking character, of political power in the modern world. And looking at the Philippine embassy, and also the Russian embassy, I thought of the transitory character of power. And

I found myself reflecting again on the words, "God guarantees the impermanence of the unjust order."

Proceeding across Massachusetts Avenue, I came to the National Rifle Association. I walked in and looked at their literature and found one fact sheet that had this to say:

> [T]he ability to effectively combat restrictions on firearms ownership is due primarily to the efforts and support of the NRA's nearly 3 million members. . . . When restrictive "gun control" legislation is proposed, at any level, NRA members and supporters are alerted and respond with individual letters and calls to their elected officials. . . . In the 1988 general elections, the NRA spent an estimated $3.9 million [on political campaigns], with an 84% success rate.

That is *power!* One of the representatives came down and chatted with me, and I said, "Is there any kind of firearm that you feel, as an organization, ought to be controlled?" He said, "Not really." And his prescription, and that of the NRA, is if we will simply stiffen enforcement of the existing laws, that will be enough. And I found myself wondering whether the power generated in that building was impacting the "street of people" with its dreadful violence, as the NRA lobbies to preserve not simply the rights of lawful gun owners but of anybody in our society to have unlimited numbers of guns on the streets.

I crossed 16th Street to the National Education Association, another one of the heavy hitters in Washington. Its nearly two million members make it the largest employee union in the country just now, though it's not affiliated with the AFL-CIO. The people were generous in explaining what they were doing and the concerns they had, feeling good about some of their recent victories politically and not so good about other issues. They were very sporting, too. Knowing that none of their opponents were on 16th Street, they generously supplied me with literature from some of their opposition. One statement, written by a religious type in Florida, condemned the NEA for being the center of secular humanism in our society. I'm not sure that was quite fair, but it helped symbolize the fact that power is not only political and economic but also cultural in character. The power to define the character of our community in its thoughts and its values and to nurture new generations is symbolized by the NEA.

Proceeding, I came to the American Association of University Women. I don't think of that organization as having a heavy political or legislative agenda. Maybe it does, and I don't know about it. But to me it did symbolize how women have begun to come into their own in American political life. Organizations like the AAUW are part, through the years, of what has given women a greater sense of confidence and empowerment to make the enormous contributions that women have to make in our American society.

Continuing down the street, I came to the Motion Picture Association of America, another reminder of the importance of cultural power. But I did not go in. I found myself reflecting what the answer might have been if I'd asked in that building, "Is there any kind of violence on the screen that you would want to simply never happen?" I don't know what the answer would have been, but it is a reminder to me, and to all of us, that the violence on our streets in our community is reflected in extraordinary displays of violence on the television screen and on cinema screens in our society.

I continued across the street to the AFL-CIO, the center of labor power in America and one of the big actors in the international labor movement. I went upstairs to chat with the religion and labor coordinator, who happens to be a member of Foundry Church. And he spoke about the AFL-CIO legislative agenda and its concerns with various health care problems, and striker replacement, and its opposition to NAFTA.

Coming down from that building I crossed the street. Around the corner, not exactly on 16th Street but right nearby, is the Chamber of Commerce of the United States. One of the former chief counsels of the Chamber of Commerce of the United States is also a member of Foundry Church, I asked about their legislative agenda and found that in some areas they parallel the AFL-CIO, and in other areas they are almost diametrically opposed.

Well, this is a walk down 16th Street, the street of power. Did I overlook any major center of power along the way? Oh, yes, the White House, across Lafayette Park. I did not go in and ask for literature at the White House. I reflected, however, that this building, and all that it symbolizes in different sectors, is possibly, arguably, the most important center of power in the entire world. And yet as I walked back on 16th Street with its heavy-hitting political action organizations, I found myself thinking again that power not only is concentrated at the White House but also is limited and enabled by what happens at other places on 16th Street and other corridors of power in our city.

So here we have the street of power, and here we have the church at the intersection of the street of people and the street of power. Is it the business of the church to be at this intersection of power and people? Some would say not. Clearly, it is our business to be concerned about people doing works of mercy and kindness, providing symbols of hope for people whose lives are lost in wretchedness and fear. Clearly, that is the agenda of the church. But the street of power? And then I reflect that what happens on the street of power impacts massively on the street of people. The National Rifle Association is not simply serving its 3 million members, in itself a drop in the bucket of the American population. It is impacting the lives and deaths of children, men, and women on the streets of people in our society.

And what happens at the National Education Association is not simply a matter of professional concern to teachers; it impacts the educational future of our whole community, our whole society. And what happens at the AFL-CIO and the Chamber of Commerce is not simply of economic interest to workers and businesspeople; their work concerns the economic well-being of our whole community and, through us, the whole world. If we are not concerned about their activities, those power configurations can very well cancel out all our missional activities of direct service to people in need. Oh, there's a very deep connection.

But it's not simply the connection of a church building at the intersection of these two streets. The real intersection of people and power is in the life of God, God who is brooding over the hurt of the people in the streets, God who is challenging those who have responsibilities of power in this great city to take responsibility before God for the well-being of God's children. Our agenda in the church is to be a beacon light of God's presence in the world at the great intersections that draw together the currents of life in our community. How beautifully this is summarized in the scripture we read today. Let me read part of it again.

> Little children, let us love, not in word or speech, but in truth and action. (1 John 3:18)

> Speak out for those who cannot speak,
>   for the rights of all the destitute.
> Speak out, judge righteously,
>   defend the rights of the poor and the needy.
>   (Proverbs 31:8–9)

And then the vision of Zechariah for the beautiful city of God:

> Thus says the Lord of hosts: Old men and old women shall again sit in the streets of Jerusalem, each with staff in hand because of their great age. And the streets of the city shall be full of boys and girls playing. (Zechariah 8:4–5)

Borrowing from the Future

Most American churches, as self-supporting institutions, must worry annually about the church budget and some sort of pledge campaign. Clergy (myself included) often feel awkward asking for money. We understand the necessity, though, in order to keep the institution afloat and to help people become better stewards. But this is not easily related to the church's prophetic message. In my Pledge Sunday sermon of October 29, 1995, I sought to set the immediate institutional concern in a much wider frame of reference: our whole relationship to the future. The prophetic insight is that faith in God transforms our attitude toward the future. That includes the future of the institutional church as a servant of God in a troubled world; it also includes environmental concerns, organ donorship, and other matters that might seem far removed from the mundane business of funding the church budget.
(Readings: Psalm 37:3–6, 21–26; 1 Timothy 6:17–19)

"The wicked borrow, and do not pay back, but the righteous are generous and keep giving." The wicked borrow and do not pay back. The righteous are generous and keep giving. That theme is the contrast between two radically different attitudes toward life: Taking from the future, consuming the future, undermining the future versus investing in the future, giving in the future, meeting God in the future. The contrast is a very important one. When I think of borrowing from the future, I am given to say that this really represents the psalmist being euphemistic. The wicked borrow and do not pay back. Well, what does it mean to borrow and not pay back? That's actually stealing, isn't it? It reminds me of one of my favorite expressions, which is a little sardonic: "I shall be forever indebted to you—because I have no intention of ever paying you back." There are people who approach life like that. I shall be forever indebted to the future, because I'm not going to pay the future back.

This is a little like the expression that I've sometimes seen on car bumper stickers, usually well-appointed cars, that says something to the effect that "We are spending our children's inheritance." Now that is a spiritual issue, through and through. I came upon a quotation some time ago from a British economist that illustrates just how deeply spiritual the issue is—though I don't think he was intending to say it was spiritual. Listen to this quotation from the economist:

> Suppose that, as a result of using up all the world's resources, human life did come to an end. So what? What is so desirable about an indefinite continuation of the human species, religious convictions apart? It may well be that nearly everybody who is already here on earth would be reluctant to die, and that everybody has an instinctive fear of death. But one must not confuse this with the notion that, in any meaningful sense, generations who are yet unborn can be said to be better off if they are born than if they are not.[3]

Note the revealing line, partly unintended: *"religious convictions apart."* Of course! Religious convictions mean convictions about what is ultimate, about what matters. Which means, What matters in the long run? That is a spiritual question. In the New Testament reading, we get something of the same theme:

> As for those who in the present age are rich, command them not to be haughty, or to set their hopes on the uncertainty of riches, but rather on God who richly provides us with

everything for our enjoyment. They are to do good, to be rich in good works, generous, and ready to share, thus storing up for themselves the treasure of a good foundation for the future, so that they may take hold of the life that really is life.

Borrowing from the future and not paying back versus giving to and for the future—a deeply spiritual issue. As a matter of fact, it's profoundly biblical. Reading the Old Testament, for example, how often you run into the issue of one's inheritance and one's children. In that agricultural society everything depended upon inheriting the land, and therefore land was passed down from generation to generation. It was a person's portion in Israel. It was a sacred trust. You had stewardship responsibility for it, to pass it on to the next generation. That is why some of the Levitical laws are so clear about the need to care for the land, to let it lie fallow at periodic intervals, so it can be restored and recovered. Even in the New Testament, where the theme doesn't appear in exactly that way, it's very interesting to look through the cracks, here and there, to see just how important that future orientation is. I think of one that might not have occurred to you (it didn't to me), and that's the parable of the prodigal son.

The point of the parable of the prodigal son is God's love, but notice the illustration: One son, the younger son, goes to his father and asks for his inheritance, which he then proceeds to waste in riotous living. Now, what could that inheritance have been? His father would have had to sell off part of the ancestral inheritance, to give him the liquid assets, the money, to take and spend in the far country. And that was offered by Jesus as a parable of just how deep God's forgiving love is, forgiving even the most grievous kind of a misuse of resources, those resources that have been passed down from generation to generation and are the legacy we are to provide for the future.

This theme is very complex and very biblical. It comes to us in a rather special way as we think of how we relate to parents and children. It's not so unusual for a parent to say, particularly in a moment of unusual stress, "How did I ever get into this? If I had even the glimmering of an idea of what this was going to lead to, would I ever have made the decision to become a parent?" That's usually said in a fleeting moment—a moment that can last more or less long. In the end, far more often those same parents will say, "What a wonderful, wonderful gift it has been to nurture this young life into youth and adulthood!" and "What a deep investment in God's future this is!"

The same theme occurs in other kinds of ways. In our own church we have people who've recently benefited from organ transplants. The other day my wife received a letter from a dear friend of hers in Colorado who, a few months ago, received a liver transplant. To understand the story fully, you need to know it was the second try. The first one didn't work. The second liver transplant, absolutely necessary for her to live, took, and she has a whole new life. It was possible for her to make contact with the donor's family, not directly but through the agency, anonymously. So she wrote the donor's family a very touching letter of thanks, saying what had happened. And this letter came back to her:

> Dear Recipient and Family,
> Thank you so much for the kind letter and card. My mother's organ donation is the only salvation for my family. To hear that it was a successful transplant made me cry. I know that my mom will live for a long time to come. The enclosed poem is why my mother chose to donate. She was fifty-three years old and the most giving person in the world. Her favorite things were sweets, movies, her grandchildren (fourteen of them), and angels. My prayers are with you and your family. Please feel free to write in the future as we would love to know how you are doing. God bless you all.

This little poem was enclosed, called "A Donor's Poem":

> [D]o not call this my "deathbed." Call it my "bed of life," and let my body be taken from it to help others lead

fuller lives. Give my sight to a man who has never seen a sunrise, a baby's face, or love in the eyes of a woman. Give my blood to the teenager who has been pulled from the wreckage of his car, so that he might live to see his grandchildren play. . . . Explore every corner of my brain. Take my cells, if necessary, and let them grow so that someday a speechless boy will shout at the crack of a bat and a deaf girl will hear the sound of rain against her windows. . . . If you must bury something, let it be my faults, my weaknesses, and all prejudice against my fellowman. Give my soul to God. . . . If by chance you wish to remember me, do it with a kind deed or word to someone who needs you. If you do all that I have asked, I will live forever.[4]

The gift of an organ is a very personal thing, a very personal kind of decision. It's something that families agonize over. I encourage it, but I understand when people feel they cannot do it. But what an eloquent testimony, not borrowing from the future but giving to the future, a very personal gift of something of one's life for others who will continue to live.

I don't think there is anything more important for a civilization than this theme of investing in the future, giving for the future. It certainly appears in the attitudes we take toward children. I find myself reflecting, as I think about this theme: One of the most important decisions of our society was made back in the nineteenth century, state by state, until all states were included, that we would not tolerate any child's not having free access to public education. Some might be educated in private schools, most in public schools, but education would be a universal thing in our society. How richly that has blessed our country! Certainly it has economically, but we have also benefited, in cultural and spiritual ways, in that deep investment in the life of the future. And today we think of other aspects of preparing our children. Nothing our society does is more important than its investment in children.

We've become newly sensitive to environmental questions: What will the character of the world as a sustaining environment be, in the long, long future? We know more about history. I'm told that if you were to take the whole history of the world and think of it as a trip around the world, humanity got on board in the last six or eight miles, and industrial civilization appeared only in the last eight minutes. Our presence on this earth is very, very recent. What are we going to do with this beautiful planet? By our best reckoning, it can last another billion years, barring external catastrophes that nobody could predict. Will there be another billion years, a vast, incomprehensibly vast, increase in the span of human life on earth, or will we, in a few short centuries, undermine the possibility of future generations? We struggle with those issues. We struggle here in the church as we reflect upon them. How very important those issues are as, good stewards, we reflect upon the future.

So now we come to our Pledge Sunday, the time when, as a congregation, we bring forth our gifts and our pledges, symbols of our loyalty, and with them our very being. A little symbol of that occurred yesterday. We had the blood drive downstairs, and quite a number of you showed up to give blood. When I was down there, I heard somebody say sardonically, "This is very appropriate that we would have a blood drive the day before Pledge Sunday! So now—will you pledge the gifts of your prayers, your presence, your service, your gifts, and your blood?" Well, there is something of our lifeblood in the pledges. They have to do with our financial gifts; they have to do with our gifts of service. Maybe, beneath it all, pledging has to do with our commitment that this be a church, and a presence of God's kingdom here in the city, to minister to all. It may be a little presumptuous for us to say that a gift to the church, of service or money, is automatically a gift to God. I know all too well that any church will misuse some of its gifts. And we're no exception. We do our best. We struggle. God is greater than we are. We're not always obedient to God. And yet, when I think about the life of this church, and of many churches, I'm not apologetic in saying there is no commitment a person can make on earth that is more clearly related to God's purposes than the kinds of commitment we make to our church.

I think of commitment to the young, to the educational and youth programs—how very important it is to nurture the life of children and youth in the faith. What an investment in the leadership of the church for generations to come, that there be in each generation those who will be raised up for the next generation, to bear witness to what Christ has done for all!

I think of the mission life of our church, often reaching out to people who are hungry and homeless, without shelter, who need medical care—being servants of Christ, ministering to the physical needs of people, helping them, without any question of whether they are Christian, or accept themselves as Christian, but rather with the clear message: "These things we are doing out of our caring love, and you can understand that these things we bring are God's gifts to you." That is an investment in God's future, as is seeing people who are spiritually, psychologically, or socially wounded, even crushed, whose lives have been in disarray, come into the life of the church and find redemption and restoration. And to reflect that whenever a person is redeemed and restored, a new future has been born. A new future has been born!

And think of the vibrant worship life of a congregation, set down in the midst of a great city, a sometimes troubled city, in a troubled world. What does it mean to Washington, D.C., and the nation, and the world, that we're here and we're doing what we do and seeking to be faithful to God, here, in this place? If you want a metaphor, go outside the church at the end of the service and look at the building next door. It's an eight-story building, recently occupied by many, many families. There were problems. The building is now boarded up, a symbol of deterioration in the city. It will not remain that way, we will see to that. But at the moment it's a symbol of deterioration, a boarded-up building. Just think if this *church* were the boarded-up building. This one! If this were not a presence in the midst of our city, what a great gaping hole there would be, what a loss to the city. We are here as a community of very diverse people, helping to demonstrate how people can get along and, more, not just get along but move along in the Spirit. We are a symbol to the world that life doesn't have to be a series of frustrations and ruinous conflicts. It's possible for people to live together and to work together as a family of God. We are a symbol of that, here.

Another metaphor, as we reflect upon our moment of commitment: We had to replace the roof. People who've been around a while know that. The original roof was put on this building when it was built in 1904. That is to say, the roof they put on this building ninety years ago was built so it would last for ninety years. That's a long time for a roof. And the decision of the church this year as we replaced the roof was, If the people of 1904 could be thinking about us in 1995, when we replace that roof we're going to be thinking about people in 2085, ninety years from now. We replaced the roof with the same kind of lasting material. We are here to stay. We are a community of Christ, here in this city, to stay and to radiate all of the love we can radiate that comes to us from God, in this city, in this place.

From Mourning to Dancing

The bombing of the Federal Building in Oklahoma City occurred during the week after Easter, 1995. The great loss of life
and the many injuries were accompanied by profound national
shock. I was out of town the following Sunday, but as I returned
to the pulpit on April 30 it was evident that we all needed to focus on the event and its implications. I almost abandoned my
previously scheduled plan to preach on the line from Psalm 30,
"You have turned my mourning into dancing." Had this, in the
aftermath of what happened in Oklahoma City, become almost
frivolous? But then, in the light of Easter—itself the turning of
tragedy into victory—it may have been exactly the right kind of
text. The bombing had also had a sobering effect on public opinion. For years the airwaves had been saturated by mean-spirited
extremism. The bombing led many people to see the relationship between such extremism and the loss of civility in public
life, and I felt it important to touch upon that relationship in this
sermon.
(Readings: Psalm 30; Revelation 5:11–14)

I usually plan my sermons, at least the titles, main themes,
and scripture lessons, about a year in advance, and so it is that
the title for this day's sermon was fixed upon nearly a year
ago, for the post-Easter period. It was taken from the lec-
tionary reading for the day, Psalm 30, which we have recited
together. One line in that psalm came leaping out to me:
"You have turned my mourning into dancing." It struck me

that while it is an Old Testament text, it encompasses what we mean by Easter. "You have turned my mourning into dancing." But, all this was long before the Oklahoma City bombing. In light of that, I struggled with the question, Is this quite right for today? "You have turned my mourning into dancing." Into *dancing*? You may wonder about that, but bear with me.

The psalm itself comes from we know not exactly what period of Hebrew history. It may have come out of a period of national grief and mourning, for there were many such times in ancient Israel. Some scholars of the Old Testament think that possibly it was a psalm of celebration to dedicate the temple as it was reconstructed in Jerusalem after the trauma of the great exile, when all had been lost, and now the Israelites were returning with joy—"you have turned my mourning into dancing." It may have been an occasion like that. There were many occasions like that in Hebrew history. Or it may not have been a particular historical context like that because mourning is universal throughout all human experience. We all sorrow and deal with suffering and tragedy and evil and death. And so those words might have been addressed out of the struggle of one person dealing with personal issues. We don't know for sure.

I find myself thinking, By what right could the ancient Israelites have spoken about dancing in light of all of the tragedy that had befallen Israel? And yet they were convinced it was God who takes up all of our quandaries and all of the evil and grief in our society and in our souls and replaces it with joy. There is a struggle there. You may have noted the words in that psalm which, in a way, I chuckle over. At first there is a moment of shaking the fist at God— How could you do this to us?—and then comes a time of turning around and, with joy, celebrating. Listen to these words from that psalm: "To you, O Lord, I cried, and to the Lord I made supplication: 'What profit is there in my death, if I go down to the pit? Will the dust praise you?'"

God, if you want me to keep on praising you, you've got to keep me alive! Then: "You have turned my mourning into dancing."

For Christians, this is resurrection, this is Easter. Out of the deepest despair, out of the pit, out of the slime, out of the hate, out of the evil, out of the sin and corruption of spirit, resurrection, Christ. God in God's power and love lifting us. That is Easter, that is resurrection. That speaks to our spirit. Isn't it remarkable, as you look around, to see people who respond in this way?

I have a picture in my mind of the great Archbishop Desmond Tutu of South Africa—actually, two contrasting views. The first one we used to get on television: Here is Archbishop Tutu in the grip of the struggle against apartheid, going out into the streets with mobs at great personal risk to stop the necklacing, that awful, awful thing, and try to rally his people around a different vision of grace and hope and possibility—the kind of action that would transform human history. The other picture is one I have seen personally both in Africa and here: that dear Archbishop preaching with such joy, even dancing in the pulpit. Can you imagine *me* doing that? It comes from within. Here is Archbishop Tutu dancing in the midst of all of the tragedy and the suffering and the sadness.

I have a picture of the Holocaust, that terrible evil. This week was the week of Holocaust Remembrance Day, and I was involved in a service the other day with a rabbi friend. He shared with me a paragraph out of a contemporary Jewish prayer book that includes a number of anecdotes about the Holocaust, and I want to share it with you. It's from the diary of Leib Lankfust, quoted in this prayer book, and it's an eyewitness account of what happened as some Jews were brought together and exterminated.

"We witnessed the arrival of transports from Binden and Sozmolek. An elderly rabbi was among them. As they came from nearby towns, they knew what was awaiting them.

They knew. The rabbi entered in the undressing room, and suddenly he began to dance and to sing all alone. The others said nothing. And he sang and he danced for a long time. And then he died for Kiddish Hashem."[5]

He died, in other words, for the sanctification of the name and the glory of God. Out of that comes rebirth and dancing.

We come to Oklahoma City. Are these words of Psalm 30 a cruel mocking of the immense tragedy that has seared the consciousness and the conscience of the nation? With such mournful grief about what happened there, we've been drenched in images. The ones that speak most to me, and I suspect to you, are the images of the children, their little baby pictures. The ones who died. The ones who survived with wounds. The ones who lost their mommies and daddies. The children. I shouldn't wonder if there were children across the land who asked, in their way, the deeper theological questions: How could this be? How could people be so *mean*? Does God let these things happen? Does God make these things happen? How hard it is in faith to be able to say, No, God does not make these things happen. God grieves along with us. God cares along with us. God has given us the kind of freedom that some people misuse in this way, and with great tragedy. God does not make this happen.

Oklahoma City. I thought of a strange little paradox about that. Have you? What do you think of when you take the word Oklahoma and drag it out? Ok-la-ho-ma. Don't the lyrics of the great Rodgers and Hammerstein *Oklahoma* flood into your mind, including references to the beauty of the morning and optimistic feelings? The songs, the joy. Did you know that Oscar Hammerstein, who wrote those joyful words, although a native-born American, was of German ancestry and had many relatives who died in the Holocaust? To sing like that, in the midst of such human tragedy, and you change mourning into dancing.

Can Oklahoma City still dance? Can America still dance? We struggle over the meaning of this, we ponder the deeper implications. These are moments that cause us to look deeply within our national soul. What's going on in this wonderfully favored land of ours? Blessed by material abundance beyond imagination. Blessed by streams of people who have come to these shores from across the world and have blended into the fabric of a society in which there can be mutual caring and mutual enrichment. The other day I heard a speech, by a grandson of Mohandas K. Gandhi, about Gandhi's attitude toward America. He had enormous appreciation for America. Gandhi used a phrase I found very interesting. He said America is unique in that this is a nation not based on bloodlines, by which he meant that this is a nation of many peoples gathered together. What a gift to the world! And what has happened?

Well, as we reflect more deeply in the aftermath of this kind of thing, I wonder why there is such grieving in our society *about* our society. What's going on more deeply under the surface? Is there not a deeper grieving? In part, it may be sadness over the economic difficulties many people have. But maybe there is a deeper kind of grieving, a mourning that people are not even quite aware of, of the loss of fellow feeling. A loss of community consciousness and public spirit, and of constructive dialogue that gathers a people together in wholeness where disagreements can enrich and not diminish and destroy. Is there not, underneath it all, a grieving for that? A sense that we're not quite right, it's not quite together? Those angry voices that fill the airwaves and the pages of all too many newspapers—in contrast to very responsible journalists and media people— Those angry voices make you want to say, Why, why be so irresponsible? You have such gifts, why not use them for the greater good? Why let your life be so contorted by hatred, by fear? What are you mourning? Can there be dancing in America?

In spite of the tragedy and the mourning, I sense some

turnings. I sense in the aftermath of this awful event in Oklahoma City a deeper pondering of the nation's soul by the nation's people. We have been given superb leadership in this by our President, who has, in this situation, been like a pastor to the nation. How badly we need that. And we have been served by leaders in both parties who have set aside their differences and acknowledged together that our common vision as a people, our being a community of mutual caring, is vastly more important than any partisan issue or partisan gain. I sense a new appreciation of that, a new struggle with that. We're also being led in that by the good people of Oklahoma City themselves. What a terrible thing happened to them, and yet we hear stories coming out of Oklahoma City that are Easter. That are about Christ's resurrection among us. A really interesting account about First United Methodist Church of Oklahoma City appeared in the *United Methodist Reporter,* the national newspaper of the church:

> Sunday's service [which means last Sunday] was a service of sorrow. "Beloved," said Rev. Nick Harris, the Senior Pastor, "for these three days, it has looked grim. It is grim, but I tell you this, First United Methodist Church will rise from the rubble. We will rise up a new and stronger church. We aren't going anywhere. We will stay in downtown Oklahoma City." With that affirmation, greeted by cheers and applause, the worship became also an effort at forgiveness and reconciliation. And so they prayed for the injured, for the volunteers who rescued them, for the dead and the missing and their loved ones, and for the bombers, whoever they might prove to be. As the voices of the crowd of nearly 1,000 swelled with lyrics of faith, people wept unashamedly in both grief and gratitude.

Dear friends, that's Easter alive and well among us. Look for all those many evidences of renewal and life in our community. Look for all the love that pours forth, bringing evidence of God's love in the risen Christ among us. We sang, already, the "Lord of the Dance," one of my favorite hymns. You sang these words:

From Mourning to Dancing

I danced on a Friday and the sky turned black;
it's hard to dance with the devil on your back;
they buried my body and they thought I'd gone,
but I am the dance and I still go on.

They cut me down and I leapt up high,
I am the life that'll never, never die;
I'll live in you if you'll live in me;
I am the Lord of the Dance, said he.

God bless Oklahoma City. May it find healing and renewal. God bless the children, may they dance with the angels in heaven. God bless our land. May it find a new birth. God bless the churches. May we be signs of reason and hope, and reconciliation and love, and of the Resurrection.

The Deep Basis
of Tolerance

October 1, 1995, was World Communion Sunday. It was also two days before the church's administrative board was to decide whether Foundry should become a "reconciling congregation." In United Methodist parlance, a reconciling congregation publicly affirms its welcome to homosexual persons. The matter had been studied by the church for five years. My sermon, based upon the Gamaliel story in Acts 5, emphasized tolerance as an open attitude toward people who are not fully understood—noting instances in the past where popular prejudices (including some held by the church) have proved to be wrong.
(Readings: Isaiah 45:1–7; Acts 5:27–39)

Today's New Testament lesson is one of the most interesting accounts in the life of the very earliest church. The disciples, the apostles, were gathered around, not very many in number. They were finally energized on Pentecost. They went out to preach. Immediately they were controversial. They continued to preach openly. The religious authorities were not amused. The apostles were arrested and hauled before the Sanhedrin. The Sanhedrin was a kind of combination Supreme Court and Congress for the Jewish nation. The expectation was that the apostles probably would not leave with their lives. In the midst of the events, the absolute outrage of the members of the Sanhedrin, one Gamaliel, known to us from independent sources as one of the great rabbinic figures of the time, stood up and offered a bit of wise counsel. In part, he said to them, "Fellow Israelites, consider carefully what you propose to do to these men. . . . [I]n the present case, I tell you, keep away from these men and let them alone; because if this plan or this undertaking is of human origin, it will fail; but if it is of God, you will not be able to overthrow them—in that case you may even be found fighting against God!" They listened to him and they let the apostles go, taking care to beat them first and to instruct them not to preach anymore—which instruction they did not follow.

Gamaliel, this great figure, was, incidentally, the first of the great rabbis to be referred to as Rabbon, which meant "our master, our teacher" to the whole nation of Israel, a person greatly respected. We know him as a Pharisee who was very liberal. He helped to modify some of the laws having to do with Sabbath observance. He was involved with efforts to liberalize some of the laws governing women, so they would have more rights in divorce proceedings. Quite an interesting figure, Gamaliel. Maybe he has something to teach us about tolerance.

I'm intrigued by Gamaliel. Certainly, his attitude urging that the early Christians be tolerated was not based on a lack of conviction. It wasn't the kind of tolerance that says, "Well, nothing matters, anything goes." He had convictions. He was not at all characterized by G. K. Chesterton's remark that "tolerance is the virtue of people who don't believe anything." Gamaliel believed important things: he was deeply grounded in the covenant; he believed in God. The advice he gave the Sanhedrin was rooted in his convictions about God: Don't worry; if this thing is only of human origin, it will end. This would be, for us, a little like Victor Hugo's comments about why Napoleon lost the battle of Waterloo. After tracing possible reasons, Hugo concluded Napoleon lost because he bothered God! These little movements will fail if they are only of human origin. But, on the other hand, if things are of God, there isn't anything you can do to make them fail. And look out. If you are running against God's purposes, you are opposing God.

Now, this is all very interesting. There is an irony in this, isn't there? If you think of Gamaliel as having saved the apostles, we realize that maybe he had it in his power, along with the rest of the Sanhedrin, to wipe out Christianity! At least we get the implication, as the story appears in Acts, that they were all there—all the apostles. Gamaliel could at least have destroyed the leadership of the very earliest Christian church! The irony is that, as we look at church history, we recognize how often Christians have repaid Gamaliel with anti-Semitism and pogroms and ultimately genocide, though I blush to think of such things as being in any sense Christian. No, Gamaliel exuded a spirit of compassion, of caring, of tolerance. He didn't refer to the kinds of movements in history that have prevailed in spite of the unlikelihood of success because of God's presence, but he might well have taken note of our Old Testament scripture reading today from Isaiah 45. The reference there is to King Cyrus, the emperor of Persia: not a Jew, but the emperor of the most powerful empire on earth at that time. Isaiah 45 speaks of Cyrus as being God's anointed. That's almost messianic language. God's anointed is Cyrus, not a Jew, doing God's purposes on earth. Then that passage goes on to speak about God as God of the whole world. God's power is universal. God's power is everywhere.

This is pretty powerful language in support of tolerance. Can we, ourselves, learn something from this? What about causes that look like they are going to win and then they lose? Can't we look back, historically, and see many movements, many of them religious movements, that appeared to be very promising, with a lot of spirit, lots of people, and yet they failed?

This week, in a completely different context, I had occasion to reread the story of the Millerites. In the first part of the nineteenth century, William Miller became convinced, as he read the Bible, the story of creation and the apocalypse, that twenty-five years from when he was reading (which was 1818, as I recall) the Second Coming was going to occur. That is, around 1843 or 1844, Christ would return and history would come to an end. As he preached about this conviction, thousands of people gathered. A lot of Methodist and Baptist churches were emptied as followers prepared for Christ's coming, and the crowds kept growing over the next twenty-five years. Eighteen-forty-three arrived, and then 1844. You don't need to feel suspense about the outcome; it didn't happen. Instead there came what was known to Millerites as the "great disappointment." There was a lot of discussion about the "great disappointment," and much theologizing about it. Out of it, in fact, some important contemporary movements have occurred—long after the disappointment itself. Here was something that appeared to have steam behind it, but in the end the movement's own expectations were not met.

Some may remember what was called the "Death of God Movement" in the 1960s. Numerically speaking, it was not much of a movement. Three or four theologians became excited about the "Death of God," and they repeated some nineteenth-century theological ideas. For a brief time this attracted the attention of the newsmagazines and a certain number of trendy people. I'm sure God was quite amused. What came of it? Well, on the positive side, a little more popular reflection on the meaning of God. But of course God remained quite secure, and the movement died.

Remember the 1970s and the sexual revolution, with its experimentation, promiscuity, and new patterns of family life that were not stable, caring relationships at all? The relationship between sexuality, caring, and commitment weakened and dissipated. Now we are seeing a return to the belief that sex needs to be expressed in caring, committed relationships. Sexuality needs to be a support for commitment and caring, not the erosion of commitment and caring. There remain difficult unresolved issues related to sexuality.

One could say that out of that period in the 1970s there were some insights, some helpful new understandings of human sexuality. But the extreme claims and behavior of that time didn't really amount to anything in the end.

Things come and go. Following the advice of Gamaliel, we will understand this process and not be too exercised over what might appear, at the moment, to be the wave of the future. On the other hand, we can observe that some things that do *not* appear to be the wave of the future, really are. Can you reflect with me on things that have not at first appeared to be of God but turned out to be?

Some of the things about which we are very sure today are the opposite of what people were very sure about yesterday. Sometimes what people thought was God's will now seems clearly not to have been God's will. For most of Christian history, Christians believed in slavery. There are scriptural texts in support of slavery: "Slaves, obey your earthly masters, . . . not . . . in order to please them, but as slaves of Christ (Eph. 6:5–6)." Today, after the struggles of the nineteenth century, the antislavery movement and the great Civil War, we are very sure that slavery is not only wrong but that slavery has always been wrong.

Similarly, the attitude toward women for most of Christian history was that women were in a subordinate place, and there are biblical passages that support this attitude: Women are to be seen and not heard. Women are not to speak in church. Possibly, women can play the organ in church, and they can sing, but they must not speak! Above all, women are not to be ordained—most of the Christian church still believes that. We know it is wrong. We know, my friends, that it has *always* been wrong! God never intended that women be secondary to men. I just hope God doesn't intend men to be secondary to women!

Throughout history, God has been at work in ways we didn't quite understand. Be careful, God may be at work! Take, for instance, the civil rights movement, that great struggle of the twentieth century. Remember that for so long people, including many Christians, thought skin color was a code for value or status. I can remember reading the words of a liberal theologian—if I can call him that today—who at the Methodist General Conference of 1936 supported a segregated system in the church at that time, saying, "God made the races separate and intended to keep them separate." What then appeared to be true we now know was not true, and was never true.

Some of the things about which we are now very clear are the opposite of things that were very clear to people yesterday. Can we draw a conclusion from that? Can't we just draw the conclusion that maybe we don't know everything? It pays to be a little tentative and to wait for the Spirit to tell us with certainty, and to be aware that God can do a new thing among us. I'm appalled that so many people think of the church not in terms of tolerance but as the main support for intolerance. I don't think that is appropriate. I think the deep message of the Christian faith is closely akin to tolerance. The deep message of the Christian faith is to accept and receive people. The deep message of the Christian faith is humility before almighty God. The deep message of the Christian faith is that the Christian church should be an oasis of tolerance in a world of intolerance.

And so what does this say to us? I suppose it says we shouldn't sweat the little stuff. We shouldn't get too exercised over small matters, the kinds of things that may be more amusing to God than of great concern. Be tolerant over the flaws we find in one another. Be open to others. I think it says to us, Remember that God is big. Don't let your God be too small. God is bigger than all of us. Whenever I interact with some of our critics—including once or twice when we've had folks demonstrating outside our church, and I found myself interacting with those who are very, very sure about us—I find myself asking, Well, what are *your* biggest doubts, what are *your* greatest uncertainties? Anybody who can't answer that question is already a fanatic!

That also leads to the question posed by a member of this

church the other day, who said, "I have the biggest difficulty being tolerant toward the intolerant." Well, we've *got* to be tolerant toward the intolerant. This will point us straight toward the central message, which is love. That God who is bigger than all of us, that God who can pour forth with new light in every generation, sheds that eternal light which we have in Jesus Christ, the light of grace and love. We need to be very tender with one another. Human beings can be so fragile, so vulnerable. We need to be caring and loving persons, recognizing that God through us can speak to others an affirming word: We love you, Christ loves you.

It is fitting that we should celebrate these words on World Communion Sunday, because on this Sunday we are reminded again that Christ has called us to a table that is universal and that encompasses the diversities of the world, a table that does not consider diversity a burden but a gift. Recognizing, as a church, that we are diverse and are enriched by our diversity in all of these things, I never cease to rejoice over this church. This beloved Foundry Church. We're not always right about everything. We fuss and we fume and we struggle. But we are a diverse congregation, and there is a lot of love here.

The Vocation of Politics

As I noted earlier in this book, it has been my practice to preach an "election" sermon every other year at the time of congressional and presidential elections. Preparation for that sermon in 1996 had special relevance. Both major presidential candidates, President Clinton and Senator Dole, had been identified with this church, although Senator Dole had by that time terminated his relationship with Foundry. I did not consider it proper for such a sermon to take sides. Rather, it was a time for sober reflection on the importance of the vocation of public service and the responsibilities of citizenship in a nation where citizens ultimately decide who is to govern. I scheduled this sermon fairly early—August 25—to help stimulate interest in the campaign and to encourage restraint and civility in the way it would be conducted.
(Readings: 1 Kings 8:22–30, 52–53; Romans 12:1–8)

We have from time to time this year given special focus in our services to Christian vocation—the calling we have from God. There is a general calling, which is to respond to God's grace. There are also specific callings, unique to each of us, in which we are called to a special form of discipleship, to respond in particular ways to the needs of the world in the service of God. The idea of calling is summarized beautifully in the passage from Romans 12 that was read a moment ago. Here again are some of those words: "I appeal to you therefore, brothers and sisters, by the mercies of God, to present your bodies as a living sacrifice." The allusion here is, of course, to the sacrifice of animals, and Paul's idea is that we are a *living* sacrifice—giving ourselves "wholly and acceptable to God, which is your spiritual worship." Paul admonishes us not to be "conformed to this world, but be transformed by the renewing of your minds," adding that "by the grace given to me I say to every one among you not to think of yourself more highly than you ought to think, but to think with sober judgment." Paul's message is about how we respond to God by giving ourselves.

And so the question is, Can you apply this message to the vocation of politics? Present your bodies as a living sacrifice, do not be conformed to this world, do not think of yourself more highly than you ought to? That is the test. Is it possible to be a Christian and follow the vocation of politics? It is a good question to raise at this time of year. From time to time, as we have dealt with other vocational spheres, I have even asked for a show of hands, an indication of how many represent that particular vocational sphere. I shall not do that this morning. However, I think it would be worth some historical footnoting that this particular presidential campaign is one of the unique occasions in American history. It may be the only time when both major-party candidates for the presidency have had a close relationship with one local church. Now, you will understand why I do not choose to overemphasize that point. And yet we can linger over it for a moment, to ask about the values, the beliefs, the common experiences that transcend the political struggle, those commitments that are above the conflict. Are there such things? Can those values and beliefs help to guide the specific vocation that a Christian might have in politics?

Some would say immediately, "No way! Politics is about the raw, ugly, mean-spirited, ambitious, ambiguous struggle for power. How could the life of Christ have anything to do with that?" And yet here we are, called to have our life related to our vocation from God. Could that vocation also be politics? I have spent a good deal of my adult life as a teacher and scholar in the field of Christian ethics, giving some attention to political ethics and Christianity and politics. And I have devoted much energy and much writing over a period of quite some years to the notion that you can be a Christian and pursue a vocation in politics. But I must confess to you that with some of the examples I have seen in recent years of how people relate Christianity to politics, I begin to wonder! Was I wrong all along? And yet how could that idea be wrong? God is the God of the whole world, not just some part of it. Politics having to do with power is not intrinsically mean or vicious; it is not intrinsically self-centered. In fact, politics can be an avenue of service. Power can be a good word. Much depends on what the power is used for and how the struggle for power is conducted.

In the early years of this country, there was a custom called the election sermon in a number of colonies. Even before the Declaration of Independence and the founding of the new nation, the preachers would, at some point in the electoral season, preach a sermon at election time, not to tell people how to vote but to tell them why it mattered and why politics is part of the economy of God's purposes on earth. I came upon one of those early sermons the other day, by Charles Chauncy. It was on Electoral Responsibility, taken from the text "civil magistrates must be just, ruling in the fear of God," and Chauncy spoke about the responsibility the people had in the election of the civil council—the colonial council—in 1747. Listen to some lines from that sermon:

> It is not for yourselves only that you are empowered and called to vote in the elections of this day, but for your God, your King and your country. And you will be unjust to them all if you give your voice as moved by any considerations but those which are taken from the real characters of men, qualifying them to sit on the council board. And with you the fault will principally lie if we have not the best men in the country for counselors, men of capacity and knowledge

who are well acquainted with the nature of government in general and the constitution, laws, privileges and interests of the people in particular. Men of unquestionable integrity, inflexible justice, undaunted resolution.

And what should such people be expected to do? Well, listen to this:

Rulers should be just to promote the general welfare and prosperity of a people by discouraging, on the one hand, idleness, profligacy, profaneness, uncleanness, drunkenness and the like immoralities, which tend in the natural course of things to their impoverishment and ruin. And by encouraging, on the other hand, industry, frugality, temperance, chastity and the like moral virtues.[6]

That is the election sermon of Charles Chauncy.

I cite this as a kind of historical footnote, to show how, in the formative years of this new nation, there was a keen understanding of the vocation of politics. Those who are summoned to service in the civil order have a high vocation from God. And what must that vocation mean concretely? Well, I suppose one of the things it might mean, following Paul, is that you don't take yourself too seriously and you don't allow politics to be personally consuming. Politics is not entered for the sake of your personal self-enhancement, if you are a Christian in politics; it is rather undertaken for the social good. Senator Mark Hatfield wrote a book some years ago called *Between a Rock and a Hard Place* to deal with the dilemmas and opportunities and possibilities of a Christian in politics. Listen to what he had to say:

[A]ny honest politician would have to admit to the ambition and ego that motivates his or her journey in public life. The allurement of power and honor subtly but malignantly grows within the politician, often gaining control of one's whole being before it is discovered. But service to others solely for their behalf and even entailing deep sacrifice is the true essence of leadership, the ultimate form of power.[7]

Every political figure I have known has had to struggle with that issue—or at least the best ones have struggled with it. But the allure of personal enhancement is a very subtle thing—the applause of great crowds, the numbers of votes, the public esteem in which one may be held—or, alternatively, the devastating effect of defeat.

Maybe a good test question is, Am I going into politics seeking public office for the sake of what I might *be*—or for the sake of what I might *do*? Politics is not a way of salvation, it is not a new being. Indeed, no political figure should take either defeat or victory too personally. It is the struggle to do good that really matters.

One of my favorite figures in recent American politics is the late Brooks Hays. As congressman from Arkansas, he was defeated in a stealth campaign in 1958 that hit him right at the last minute, a write-in campaign for an unknown segregationist dentist in Little Rock. They went after Brooks Hays because he was not going to support segregation. He was a very courageous man and a man of deep conviction. He was a spiritually driven man. He was, in fact, president of the Southern Baptist Convention for a term, devoted to Christ and to the church and to his calling in politics. But there was a line beyond which he would not go.

He liked to tell a story that shows his wry sense of humor about the day after that election, when suddenly he was booted out of office. He came down the stairs, greeted his wife at breakfast, and said, "Honey, I can't eat the Wheaties anymore." And she said, "Why not?" And he said, "Because that's the Breakfast of Champions!"

This may be a good test for political figures: Do you aspire to Congress (or the presidency or the city council, or some other office) for the sake of your own self-enhancement or for the sake of what you wish to do? What is more important in your life than winning? If a person can't answer that question, we're not dealing with vocation in politics.

Of course, that leads to the question, What does one want to do in politics? A political vocation requires concern about the whole society, not just some part of it. Even those people who have voted against you are still a part of the community, and you are responsible as a public servant for their well-being as well as that of those who supported you. To be a Christian in the vocation of politics is to care about society as a whole and each member in it. This reminds us that when people are asked to be loyal to their country or their community, the country and the community must be loyal to them. The country must have a deep commitment to every member in society, bar none. This poses difficult dilemmas and problems for politicians, but that underlying value of community is very important.

How does one go about embodying this belief? Well, to be involved in politics in a serious way, as a Christian, is to be at the tension point between ideals, those lofty goals that are your purpose in politics, and the need to compromise in the real world. How difficult that can be for anybody in politics who takes the responsibility seriously! Max Weber, the great German philosopher and social scientist, wrote an essay called "Politics as a Vocation." It was not a theological essay. In fact, it does not have anything in it about God or Christ, but it does speak about the dilemma between the ideal and the practical. As Weber describes it, there is, on the one hand, an ethic of ends, which is concerned with what you are to gain, and, on the other hand, an ethic of consequences or responsibilities, which is concerned with what you are actually doing. Here are some of his words:

> [I]t is immensely moving when a *mature* man—no matter whether old or young in years—is aware of the responsibility for the consequences of his conduct and really feels such responsibility with heart and soul. He then acts by following an ethic of responsibility, and somewhere he reaches the point where he says: "Here I stand, I can do no other." That is something genuinely human and moving. . . . [A]n ethic of ultimate ends and an ethic of responsibility are not in absolute contrast, but rather supplements, which only in unison constitute a genuine person, a person who can have the calling for politics.[8]

Those words are worth pondering, as we recognize that all great figures in politics have had to struggle with the tension between the highest goals, the lofty goals, on the one hand and the need to compromise on the other. It means that political figures often disappoint people at either end of the spectrum. The inner issue of integrity is something each person must confront in his or her own spiritual life.

There is another political figure from Arkansas of some years past whom I admired immensely for his vision in dealing with foreign affairs: Senator J. William Fulbright, responsible for the Fulbright scholarship program, but who signed on to the Southern Manifesto in support of segregation in the 1950s. I was deeply disappointed by that act, both then and now. I question his judgment, but I don't question his basic integrity. I think his concern was the role he might play as an effective presence in international relations, and the Southern Manifesto was the price he felt he had to pay in his own home political base. That's the struggle one must undertake—between the ideal and the practical. And then, of course, it has to do with how you conduct the struggle for power.

We have, throughout the history of this country, had a lot of mean-spirited demagoguery in our politics. You know Aristotle's main concern about democracy back in early Greece was that it would lead to demagoguery—and I think every democratic society provides some proof of the warning. But in recent years it seems to me that the demagoguery, the mean-spiritedness, the character assassination have gone further. I pause over that a bit, knowing that even some of the greatest figures in American public life have had to suffer some kind of vilification. Take, for instance, criticism of Abraham Lincoln—to cite the person most of us would regard as one of the two or three greatest American presidents. Listen to what one historian wrote about the difficulties he faced:

> From the day of his inauguration to the day of assassination, the invective was unrelenting. Among other things, Lincoln was called an ape, a baboon, a buffoon, a clown, a usurper, a traitor, a tyrant, a monster, an idiot, a eunuch, a bigot, a

demagogue, a lunatic, a despot, a blunderer, a charlatan, and a bully. One New York newspaper regularly referred to him as "that hideous baboon." *The Illinois State Register* [that is, his home state] called him "the craftiest and most dishonest politician that ever disgraced an office in America." Even his hometown paper [that would be Springfield] joined the chorus "how the greatest butchers of antiquity sink into insignificance when their crimes are contrasted with those of Abraham Lincoln."[9]

Vilification is not new. But I remind you that that era also produced a Civil War. And, in our time, the edge of civility is always tested by methods of winning elections that in fact destroy community. The responsibility of vocational politics for a Christian is to come to the end of a campaign with the life of the community enhanced and not degraded by the way in which the campaign was conducted.

I am pleased that both of the major party candidates for the presidency have in one way or another underscored that theme in this year. And I trust that they and others who are like-minded will help to keep this a more elevated campaign season than some of those we have had in recent years. But do you know where the final responsibility for that lies? With us. I have spoken about the vocation of politics as though it is a vocation for the politicians. It is, but it's also a vocation for the citizens. We are the ones who set the parameters and ultimately determine the outcomes. If attack ads are used, it's because they are effective. And who determines their effectiveness? It's you and I who respond to them. If we send a signal very clearly that we will have none of that, if we insist on a campaign that addresses issues and exemplifies mutual respect and fosters mutual trust in a community of people, then that kind of campaign will be the result. If we insist on a campaign that does not involve sectarianism and where our expression of Christianity embraces all people whatever the result, that is what the result of the campaign will be. It is largely up to us.

Some years ago, George Bernard Shaw came up with an

aphorism I found interesting. He said that "while democracy may not be the most perfect form of government, it is that form of government that best guarantees that people will get what they deserve." These are perhaps unfair words for those who have fought in a minority party and lost. And yet those words are a reminder that finally it is up to us: we the people, we who have the privilege of participating in a democratic society. We are the ones who ultimately determine the shape of our politics. I pray—do you join me in this prayer?—that this campaign season in America, with all of its great stakes and all of the struggle, will be conducted in such a way that at the end it will be a blessing to this country, helping to heal us and draw us closer together as a national community.

No Bread for the Journey

Sunday, January 19, 1997, was an especially challenging time for Foundry Church. It was the day before President Clinton's second inauguration. He and the First Lady were present, along with a large number of visitors and some demonstrators outside. The mood of the city was upbeat, despite the extensive security arrangements. At the time of a presidential inauguration (and perhaps only at that time), partisan considerations are laid aside and the focus of the nation is on new beginnings.

I decided to preach on what it means to venture forth in response to God's call, trusting in God for support and direction. Since, by coincidence, this was also the weekend of the Martin Luther King national holiday, it was appropriate to speak about how the civil rights movement had had a strong sense of divine calling and a deep trust in God to see it through.

It is usually best not to call special attention to the presence of the President in a worship service. But there are occasions, such as this one, where a person in that position should be able to feel the spiritual support and love of sisters and brothers in the faith. Toward the end of the sermon, I reminded the congregation of the implications of Paul's metaphor of the Body of Christ (in which all are equal) and suggested that in a real sense we were all to be inaugurated the following day. Then I told a little story to suggest to the President and First Lady that they are in our prayers. *(Readings: Genesis 12:1–3; Luke 9:1–6)*

Today's scripture lessons have a common theme. It's the

theme of venturing forth in trust. It's a theme that runs all through the Bible, with many illustrations.

We began with the story of Abraham, at age seventy-five, leaving the security of his home, leaving everything that was familiar, and venturing forth in response to God's bidding. Venturing with the promise of land and of descendants who would be numberless as the grains of sand on the beach. We think of the story of the Exodus, the children of Israel released from captivity, going out they knew not where, and beginning to grumble because they knew not how. And manna was provided. And then we think of this marvelous recapturing of the whole biblical story in Hebrews 11, that great chapter on faith, which rehearses the stories of so many of the Hebrew heroes of the past and their ventures of faith, and concludes, "All of these died in faith without having received the promises, but from a distance they saw and greeted them. . . . For people who speak in this way make it clear that they are seeking a homeland. . . . Therefore God is not ashamed to be called their God."

Remember, too, the section of the Gospel of Luke that tells about how Jesus sends the twelve disciples forth to proclaim the kingdom of God, to heal and to teach, and to be God's presence, and with the word that they are to take nothing for their journey, "no staff, nor bag, nor bread, nor money—not even an extra tunic." Take no bread for your journey. Let's not quibble over whether that means we shouldn't plan anything. And if you're going to be on the Mall tomorrow, as I venture many will be, don't take literally that part about not even an extra tunic! This is not a prescription to stop providing, planning, and thinking about the future. The point is much more serious: When God calls, you can count on God to see you through. If God calls you, and it truly is God's call, and you're sure of it and you've tested it, and it's not just an illusion and not just a whim, and not just something self-serving, if God truly calls you, you go! Whether or not you have sandwiches for the journey, *you go!*

What Jesus was saying, really, is, "Look, go out into these villages, proclaim the kingdom of God. Heal, teach. If they receive you, it will be God's spirit receiving you. And they'll provide for you. And if they don't, here's another little word: Shake the dust of that place from your heels and walk. God will provide."

That is a hard lesson. I don't think there is anybody here today who hasn't struggled with it. Tested it and been tested by it. I remember when I went to seminary. We were not a very affluent family, my father being a country preacher. I had just enough money in hand for the train trip across the country from California to Boston, the first semester's tuition, and ten dollars. Well, I knew it was right, and I knew the church was there, and I could work, and it would happen. And I thank God that it has.

How often in our personal decisions we have to venture in faith. If we had to have all the answers before we ventured forth, most of the time we never would go. The venture of a vocation. If you're moving into some vocation that is not terribly lucrative, and where you may have years of preparation, or venturing into the decision with a life mate—if you have to have all the answers, you'll never get around to it. Or take the decision to have or to adopt children. Actually, if you knew everything that was going to happen you probably wouldn't do it. But years later, and most of the time along the way, you'll be sure it was right. If God calls, you go. Even if it means no bread for the journey.

That's a great theme for a weekend in which we celebrate Martin Luther King and the civil rights movement. The whole movement from start to finish was a journey of faith. Without bread for the journey. Some of you have seen the movie *Ghosts of Mississippi*. It tells the story of Medgar Evers, the great martyr to the civil rights movement, who carried the weight of the civil rights movement in Mississippi before there *was* a movement, and who was tragically assassinated in 1963, just moments after President Kennedy had finished his great speech on television announcing support for a civil rights law. The movie is about the vindication of Evers and the bringing to trial yet again (after twenty-five years) of the one accused of killing him. But the movie took me back to a moment when Carolyn and I visited with Medgar Evers in Jackson, Mississippi, in the summer of 1958. That's a little while ago! We visited the humble offices of the NAACP there where Medgar Evers and his wife, Myrlie Evers, were the movement, were the organization. I can't tell you a lot about the conversation. I know he spoke of the conditions, the deplorable era of segregation and terror they had to confront. But the one thing I remember specifically was when, without any histrionics, without any self-glorification, and without even a hint of wanting to be a martyr, Medgar Evers, supported by his wife, Myrlie, said to us across that humble desk, "I know this may cost my life, and I am prepared for that if it happens." Take no bread for the journey, God will provide.

God did provide through that magnificent civil rights movement, which forever has transformed this land. Encouraged by the spirit of people like Medgar Evers, and the one we especially celebrate this weekend. In 1963, a few months after the assassination of Medgar Evers, when Martin Luther King was engaged in the Birmingham movement, there was a question of whether he should spend his time in Birmingham, where he might go to jail and be removed from practical usefulness to the civil rights movement, or should instead be out in the country raising money for the cause. Most of his advisers said, "You should be out raising money." But Dr. King knew in his bones that wasn't the right answer. And he said, "I don't know what will happen. I don't know where the money will come from. But I have to make a faith act."[10] And that faith act, and the magnificent letter from Birmingham jail, captured resources and attention that one person running around the country never could have raised. It was like sparks falling on tinder. The energies of people of goodwill all over the nation focused on Birmingham, turning what was a problematic situation into a decisive moment for the civil rights movement. Take no bread for the journey.

This weekend, by coincidence, is not only Martin Luther King weekend but the weekend in which we celebrate a presidential inaugural. We think long thoughts about our national journey as a people. To some here, 220 years may seem like a very long time. But we all understand that even 220 years is not long in the vast sweep of human history. We think of this land of ours as the world's oldest democracy. In a manner of speaking, that may be so. We still honor the vision and the faith of people who carried off a revolution and a Declaration of Independence, and somehow managed to forge a Constitution that has endured for over two centuries. Somehow they developed institutions of government that could carry the weight of accumulated national experience in a vastly changing world. One does not need to romanticize that history to say it has been a truly remarkable journey on which we have been as a people.

We think long thoughts as we gather at inauguration time. There is a real sense in which we inaugurate not just two people but a whole country. It is a time of rededication, a time of celebration of what this history has meant and will mean. It is a time of commitment to the journey ahead. It's a time for thinking sober thoughts about what that might mean. Will this nation be committed to the common good, so that our understanding of the common good is translated into a broadly shared commitment by all of us? Will we be a nation in which the forms and institutions of democracy are perfected by customs of civility? Will the nation realize the dream of the civil rights movement, and implicitly the dream of the whole country—that we should be a land where brotherhood and sisterhood crown our good from sea to shining sea? Will the nation be a blessing to a world that increasingly turns to this land for resources and leadership? These questions all suggest a journey, not *from* perfection and not *to* perfection, but a journey in response to a high vision of who we are as a nation.

We do not, in the community of faith, single out any in our midst as more worthy or better than any other. In some respects, the most profound vision of the church is that wonderful concept of Paul where the church is the body of Christ in which all have functions to play. All have gifts to bring, and all, together, are honored. And that, indeed, is a conception not only of the church but of what the kingdom of God means in human life, in human society.

Nevertheless, we do acknowledge special gifts and special burdens. So, today, we acknowledge the gift of those in our midst, not unknown to us, whom we cherish and honor. We support them in the midst of those burdens. We think together as a congregation, as a church, as a people, of how important it is for those who are summoned to high leadership to know that they are supported by the prayers and goodwill of their fellow citizens, and especially of those of the community of faith who share the faith with them.

I remember a story of a Scottish preacher, a young man, who ventured out of his university experience for the first time to be the preacher in a little kirk in a village in the Highlands. He arrived a week before he was to preach for the first time, and he was visibly nervous. The people of the village noticed that and so they elected one in their midst, a village elder, to talk with him. The old man came to him and said, "Young man, you need to know that as the smoke rises from the chimneys of the village each morning, so do the prayers of the people rise for their pastor." I like the ring of that! But today we think of the one who is called again to lead the United States of America. He is not as young as that Scottish preacher, nor as young as he was four years ago. It's not the first time around! But I hope and trust that the President and First Lady understand that as the smoke rises from millions of chimneys across this land and across the world, so do the prayers for you two and for others, as you again assume these immense burdens. God bless you.

Both Conservative and Liberal

This sermon, preached January 11, 1998, sought to address the facile labeling and stereotyping of people as "conservative" or "liberal." The labels make it all too easy to dismiss views with which we are in disagreement. Views and persons who are dismissed in this way no longer have to be taken seriously. The main point of the sermon was about more than semantics. When people or groups are dismissed with such labels, the already dangerous polarization of society is increased. But society needs constructive ideas from both conservatism and liberalism. Both are well grounded biblically, a point I sought to establish early in the following sermon. The section on biblical scholarship was in the sermon for two reasons: first, to encourage members to appreciate critical biblical scholarship and not to be threatened by it; second, to anticipate the problem that some contemporary put-downs of categories of people do have biblical support but without representing the deep message of the Bible.
(Readings: Isaiah 42:5–10; Matthew 5:17–24)

Some of you may have had the same experience as I have of being identified by friendly critics as either ultraliberal or ultraconservative. (Well, I don't suppose I have often been called ultraconservative!) I don't think one should be offended by such labels. There is nothing wrong with being liberal or conservative. But one can be a little mystified by being identified in such a way. What do the labels mean? As Christians we might especially ask, What do they mean biblically?

Are you surprised to learn that neither word appears anywhere in the Bible? The word "liberal" does appear once in the Apocrypha, referring to being a liberal giver. Otherwise, there is nothing in the New Revised Standard Version of the Bible or Apocrypha about either word.

In today's language, as frequently used, "conservative" seems to mean somebody who is thinking primarily of preserving the past and its institutions and traditions. One's interest is in *conserving*. "Liberal," on the other hand, refers to an attitude of freedom and, often, change. So a liberal may be someone who is looking for change. Put simply, a conservative can be thought of as the brakes, a liberal as the accelerator. Which of these is more in keeping with our faith as Christians?

Both of today's readings from the Bible make it impossible for us to choose between the two. The Isaiah reading is about "the former things" that have come to pass. It speaks of all the Lord has done to sustain the people of Israel and to give Israel as a light to the nations. But then it goes on to speak of "new things I now declare, before they spring forth" and "Sing to the Lord a new song." It is about what God has done in the past, but it is also about new things that are yet to be.

Matthew 5, which is from the Sermon on the Mount, also has that double message. We read, "I have come not to abolish but to fulfill" the law. But then, as Jesus explains what that means, the move is clearly a deeper move into the meaning of the law, and Jesus also uses the formula "You have heard that it was said . . . But I say to you . . ." Jesus is talking about big changes in the religious outlook of the people. But the passage is not a repudiation of the traditions that have been received from the past; only about fulfilling them in new ways. It refers to the letter of the inherited law but pushes beyond it to the divine *intent* of the law—which has comparatively little to do with legalism and a lot to do with human rights and love and reconciliation. To Jesus, love and reconciliation were the very essence of the inherited law. To be a real conservative, in that sense, is to be a loving, reconciling person. But to be a real liberal is to embrace new possibilities even as we are grounded in old traditions.

Seen from this vantage point, many of the great conflicts between conservatives and liberals are misplaced. There is clear need for both.

Take biblical study, for instance. Is it liberal or conservative to accept the biblical scholarship of the past two hundred years? It may seem liberal, even dangerously liberal. Because that scholarship deals rigorously with inconsistencies within the Bible while exposing to view the way ancient cultural attitudes affected its writing, it might seem to some to be a way to destroy the influence of the Bible. As some people have said, if you can't believe every word of the Bible, exactly as written, how can you believe any of it?

But is that necessarily the really conservative attitude to take? The essence of conservatism is to preserve the best from the past, even as we look toward the future. Biblical scholarship has not destroyed the Bible for us; it has enhanced it. It helps us see the biblical message from a genuinely human perspective and to understand how it is that real human beings were deeply inspired. In the long run, people will not accept what they cannot believe to be true. It helps to know all we can about the Bible, for that helps us see what really matters in the biblical message and what doesn't. For instance, we see that we do not have to put down people who have been denigrated by parts of the Bible. We can perceive in a new way how the deeper message of God's reconciling love applies to everybody.

But then, is it necessarily liberal to treat the Bible as being only an ancient book with obsolete ideas? No. To be liberal is to be open to truth and to follow it where it leads. And much of the Bible speaks to the present time just as it did to the ancient world and helps lead us through the dilemmas of modern life. So responsible biblical scholarship can be both conservative and liberal in the deepest sense.

I would say the same thing about the social world. Is it liberal or conservative to be concerned about human rights? It is both, of course. A liberal seeks to extend the frontiers of human rights until all people are included. But the foundations of that attitude are quite ancient—including the biblical tradition and the best thought of the Greeks and Romans. We are also coming to see that there is much in non-Western traditions concerning human rights that is worthy of preservation. The American traditions based on the Bill of Rights are a legacy from the past that helps direct us toward a better future. Conservative or liberal? The two are mingled, are they not?

I began by saying that there is nothing wrong with being liberal or with being conservative. It may be truer to say that there is something wrong with not being a little bit of both. There are important values and traditions to preserve. There are new challenges to confront. We are not to abolish the legacies of the past; we are to fulfill them in ways our ancestors could not have imagined but which they would applaud if they were here to observe.

This church has struggled with such questions, and today we celebrate some of the results of that struggle. We have become a "reconciling congregation." Right along there have been different understandings of what that means in detail. But it at least means that as a church we embrace the mission of reconciling those who have been estranged from one another. And part of that mission is to embrace people who have experienced rejection in other places. That applies to people of different kinds; we made that clear in the statement we adopted in 1995. But we have all understood that it applies with special force to people of different sexual orientation. We said:

> We seek to be an inclusive congregation, and we proclaim our commitment to seek the reconciliation of all persons to God and to each other through Jesus Christ. As we journey toward reconciliation with all, we proclaim this statement of welcome to all, including our gay and lesbian brothers and

sisters. God loves you and we love you, we affirm you and accept you, we treasure you. We welcome you.

Is a statement like that conservative or liberal? It is certainly liberal, for it pushes beyond the conventional wisdom of many people. It seeks to move us all beyond destructive stigmas and stereotypes, and that includes moving beyond a narrow interpretation of the Bible. But maybe it is conservative as well. It certainly seeks to conserve the very heart and soul of biblical faith, which is about God's reconciling love, expressed through Christ. It also seeks to acknowledge and conserve the great value of people who have been condemned and hated but not understood and loved.

There is one aspect of this mission where the relationship between conservative and liberal is especially put to the test. That is the question whether the church should bless the committed unions of persons of the same gender. Many, perhaps most people, would say that this is liberal—indeed, that this is far *too* liberal. But when people stop to think more seriously, they begin to see that this may also be quite conservative as well. It certainly is a way of supporting love and commitment. In opposition to such committed unions, one member of Congress exclaimed, "The flames of hedonism, the flames of narcissism, the flames of self-centered morality are licking at the very foundation of our society, the family unit."[11] But surely he cannot be right about this. Genuine love and commitment are far removed from hedonism. This is not about seeking pleasure selfishly and for its own sake; this is about caring for another. Some family values organizations have made a kind of campaign against such unions as a way of preserving the family. But have they really thought this matter through? Isn't the essence of family life the bond of mutual care and nurturing love that people can count on and that helps them to grow?

In last Sunday's *Washington Post,* the Rev. Tom Starnes wrote feelingly about what it meant for his family to observe the Christmas holiday with their gay son and the one with whom he is in a committed relationship. He wrote about the initial shock he and some of the others in his family felt a few years ago when he learned first of his son's sexual orientation and, later, about the relationship. But then the human realities became clearer and very positive. Starnes draws us into an appreciation for the child these two men adopted:

> Keott is one of the family, too. He is the nine-year-old boy that Floyd and Carlos took in at age three and adopted just last year. Floyd and Carlos are wonderful parents. It is nothing short of amazing to watch Keott's development. To see a terrorized, apprehensive child move along the way toward becoming an open, loving, trusting child is a sight to behold.[12]

Some might find that unacceptably liberal. But is it really? "To see a terrorized, apprehensive child move along the way toward becoming an open, loving, trusting child"— isn't that also conservative, in the sense of conserving and enhancing what is very good?

The "reconciling congregation" statement that our church adopted also notes that "there remain differences of opinion among us on issues relating to sexuality" and that "we do not seek to erase our differences, but to journey together in faith toward greater understanding and mutual respect." That may be an understatement of the differences! I trust it is also an understatement of our commitment to the quest for greater understanding and mutual respect. For a congregation, drawn together in mutual faith and love, is by its nature both conservative and liberal. What were those words from Isaiah? Could they also have been addressed to us?

> I am the Lord, I have called you in righteousness,
>   I have taken you by the hand and kept you;
> I have given you as a covenant to the people,
>   a light to the nations,
>   to open the eyes that are blind,
>   to bring out the prisoners from the dungeon,
>   from the prison those who sit in darkness.
> I am the Lord, that is my name;
>   my glory I give to no other,

Speaking the Truth in Love

nor my praise to idols.
See, the former things have come to pass,
and new things I now declare. . . .
Sing to the Lord a new song,
his praise from the end of the earth.

Taking the Bible Seriously

This sermon, scheduled for January 25, 1998, was to be part of a midwinter series of sermons on the general theme of taking faith seriously. My intention for the series was to interact with the congregation on troubling issues of faith that are both intellectual and practical. How can we think and act responsibly on the basis of Christian faith? The first sermon, the previous week, was "Taking God Seriously." This one, on the Bible, was largely intended to be an exploration of major issues in biblical thought. Can honest people, facing the difficulties exposed by biblical scholarship, still find the basis of their faith in this ancient book? The sermon was not to be a lecture on the Bible, but its major focus would still be intellectual, more than practical or inspirational.

Events have a way of unhinging our best intentions. On January 22 sensational charges were made in the press, alleging that the President had behaved improperly with a White House intern and committed perjury to cover it up. The nation's media pursued the story ferociously; pundits speculated that the President could be impeached and might resign. Rumors flew around, some treated as fact by a press hungry for new developments and scoops. In that climate, it seemed to me that many of the people of Foundry Church would be in shock and grief. I was tempted, briefly, to set aside the announced sermon topic and address the issue of the moment directly. I certainly could not simply ignore it. But the more I thought about it, the clearer it seemed that the best way to take the Bible seriously was to demonstrate the Bible's relevance to the crisis at hand. In recasting the sermon, I placed less emphasis on issues of biblical scholarship and more emphasis on the deep message of the Bible. I think it was a better sermon for that, quite apart from the crisis of the moment.

(Readings: Jeremiah 31:31–34; 2 Timothy 3:14–17)

Today's sermon is the second in a series on the general theme, Taking Faith Seriously. The series is based on the importance both of our faith and of thinking about it. Last week we spoke of taking God seriously. Today, I wish to speak on what it means to take the Bible seriously. The Bible? It is the book that contains the basic foundations of our faith. I cannot imagine taking Christian faith seriously without taking the Bible seriously, because that is where the roots of our faith are to be found.

But I must confess to you that I seriously thought of changing the announced sermon topic this week in light of the events of the last week. I was tempted to say that the preferable text of the moment might be the lines from Herman Wouk's novel about World War II, *The Caine Mutiny.* In a scene of great confusion we read the sarcastic words, "When in danger or in doubt, run in circles, scream and shout." There certainly has been much of that this week.

But upon sober reflection, it seemed clear to me that taking the Bible seriously means taking it seriously as it illuminates life. A week like this helps us see just how deep and helpful the Bible really is.

So, what does it mean to take the Bible seriously? There are quite a few Christians who would answer quite simply: to take the Bible seriously is to believe it. "God said it—I believe it. That settles it." God said it in the Bible, and I believe that the words of the Bible are God's words. That is what biblical literalism means: Every word, every sentence, every page of the Bible is set forth as God intended. "God said it—I believe it."

About two centuries ago, biblical scholars began a more careful examination of scripture, applying to the Bible the kind of analysis that might be used with other forms of literature. Critical study was undertaken to establish probable authorship, dates of writing, and circumstances, to understand inconsistencies, repetitions, and other anomalies. Early in the twentieth century a major controversy boiled over between those who accepted the results of this study and research and those who did not. In the midst of this, one irate fundamentalist is supposed to have asked his pastor, "Well, do you take the Bible literally or not?" The pastor thought a moment and then replied, "No, I don't take the Bible literally. *I take it seriously.*"

Is that fair? It might not seem so. What attitude toward the Bible could be more serious than to accept every word of it as having come directly from God?

But look again. Anyone who reads the Bible, the whole Bible, very carefully will discover contradictions, different versions of the same event, claims made that stretch our credulity to the breaking point, even questionable moral teaching and radically different portraits of God. Is it possible to hold all that together in a *serious* way, really believing that it is all so?

There is a subtler problem. If every word of the Bible is exactly as God intended it, that means, does it not, that in some fashion God dictated it to the human authors? That they were, more or less, stenographers? But if the authors were only stenographers, they were not necessarily seriously engaged with the subject matter. Their function was mechanical, not substantive or creative. God spoke; they got the words right. But what about the meaning of the words? What about the *spirit* of the words?

Such a mechanical view of the Bible also puts everything on a one-dimensional basis. All on the same level. No peaks and valleys, no shades of dark and light. It's just there: Take it or leave it.

But the Bible is so much more than that! The characters in the Bible are real human beings. The writers of the Bible are real human beings. It is all about how God created us as real human beings and comes to us in our humanity.

To take the Bible seriously is not to take it literally. But it is to understand that the Bible is *inspired*. The word means "in the spirit." So much of the Bible is written by people who were touched by God's spirit. That helps us to see the parts of the Bible that are most profound—and not to worry so much about the parts that are more a reflection of a time-bound culture now past.

You don't even have to worry as much about whether everything is factual. Sometimes truth is best conveyed in a story that is not factual. Jesus knew that. A very important part of his message was contained in parables: the prodigal son, the good Samaritan, the lost coin, the workers in the vineyard. These are not presented as factual. They are presented as illustrations of deep truth about God.

We can identify with the Bible because it tells us of the struggle of humankind, through all history, to understand, do good, and know that all of us are flawed in our humanity. The Bible conveys the unvarnished truth about *that!* Here is King David, revered even now as the greatest ruler of Israel, who was very human in his flaws, very great in his strengths, above all a man of deep feeling. Here is Peter—the "rock"—but so unlike a rock. Impetuous, fickle. On the night when Jesus faced his greatest test and needed the support of his friends and disciples, where was Peter? Cowering by the fire, denying his Master three times. And later, where was Peter when the church faced its most strategic decision: Would it be open to the Gentiles? He was confused, had to be brought along. But in the end, Peter really was a rock, one of the two dominant leaders of the earliest church. And, according to tradition, he even suffered a painful death as a martyr.

And here is Paul. We first meet him as Saul of Tarsus, persecutor of Christians: arrogant, vengeful. We first meet him as an accomplice to murder—the shameful stoning of Stephen. But Christ spoke to him. Somehow he saw the depth of Christ's love and responded to it. He became the first great theologian of the church and its greatest missionary. Without him we cannot imagine how the church would have spread throughout the Roman world or how the deep insights of the faith would have been translated into language understandable to non-Jews. Even so, here is Paul, prone sometimes to impatience, acknowledging his own weakness, writing some things about women and slaves that are not consistent with his deep message. The Bible is real because it is about real people. It is profound because it is about how God touches the lives of real people.

Much of the Bible speaks directly to us in our brokenness. Read the Psalms, which often voice the despair of those who have nearly given up hope. Read, for instance, Psalm 130:

> Out of the depths, I cry to you, O Lord.
> Lord, hear my voice!
> Let your ears be attentive
> to the voice of my supplications!
>
> If you, O Lord, should mark iniquities,
> Lord, who could stand?
> But there is forgiveness with you,
> so that you may be revered.
>
> I wait for the Lord, my soul waits,
> and in his word I hope;
> my soul waits for the Lord
> more than those who watch for the morning,
> more than those who watch for the morning.

How many people there are who find night a time of special despair, who yearn for the morning—both literally and figuratively. The Bible is addressed to real people in their anguish.

I would be hard pressed to name a single favorite chapter in the Old Testament, there are so many that speak to me. But on most days, if urged, I would say that my very favorite is Isaiah 40, which speaks to the broken people of Israel in their captivity in Babylon, probably the lowest point in all

Hebrew history. Isaiah 40 speaks of the fragility of human life, of our vulnerability:

> A voice says, "Cry out!"
> And I said, "What shall I cry?"
> All people are grass,
> their constancy is like the flower of the field.
> The grass withers, the flower fades,
> when the breath of the Lord blows upon it;
> surely the people are grass.

But is that to be the last word? No. The last word is a word of hope:

> Comfort, O comfort my people,
> says your God.
> Speak tenderly to Jerusalem,
> and cry to her
> that she has served her term,
> that her penalty is paid. . . .
> Get you up to a high mountain,
> O Zion, herald of good tidings;
> lift up your voice with strength,
> O Jerusalem, herald of good tidings,
> lift it up, do not fear. . . .
> Have you not known? Have you not heard? . . .
> The Lord is the everlasting God,
> the Creator of the ends of the earth.
> He does not faint or grow weary;
> his understanding is unsearchable.
> He gives power to the faint,
> and strengthens the powerless.
> Even youths will faint and be weary,
> and the young will fall exhausted;
> but those who wait for the Lord shall renew their
> strength,
> they shall mount up with wings like eagles,
> they shall run and not be weary,
> they shall walk and not faint.

That speaks a word of hope to us in our brokenness. Of course, the Bible also addresses the world's brokenness. The great prophets of the Old Testament write with a God-inspired power that is relevant even today. They help us understand that society must be good for everybody or it is not going to be much good for anybody. They help us see that the poor and downtrodden are God's beloved, and that God is fiercely protective. They help us see that God's purpose is peace, and that God points us toward a world in which the terrors of war and oppression have been overcome.

Above all, the Bible speaks to us of love. Maybe the best short description of the Bible is to say that it is a great love story: the love of God for humankind, you and I, created by God from the dust of the earth, brought forth into the understanding of good and evil, destined for love. And the love of humankind for God and for one another.

Today's New Testament lesson, from 2 Timothy 3, asserts that "all scripture is inspired by God." That is not about biblical literalism; it is about *inspiration,* it is about scripture being in the *spirit.* When one speaks of the Bible as "inspired," don't we mean ultimately that it is inspired by the God of love and that it draws us into the spirit of love? God's Holy Spirit is an expression of pure love. The greatest moments in the Bible are about that. We all have favorite passages. I would be hard put to say which part of the Bible means most to me, for there is so much that is meaningful. And I find the Bible speaks to me now in one way, now in another. But if I had to choose just one New Testament passage, on most days I know which one it would be. And especially today, as the nation is in some spiritual turmoil, it is the one I would want everybody to hear. It goes like this:

> If I speak in the tongues of mortals and of angels, but do not have love, I am a noisy gong or a clanging cymbal. And if I have prophetic powers, and understand all mysteries and all knowledge, and if I have all faith, so as to remove mountains, but do not have love, I am nothing. If I give away all my possessions, and if I hand over my body so that I may boast, but do not have love, I gain nothing.

Speaking the Truth in Love

Love is patient; love is kind; love is not envious or boast-ful or arrogant or rude. It does not insist on its own way; it is not irritable or resentful; it does not rejoice in wrongdo-ing, but rejoices in the truth. It bears all things, believes all things, hopes all things, endures all things.

Love never ends. But as for prophecies, they will come to an end; as for tongues, they will cease; as for knowledge, it will come to an end. For we know only in part, and we prophesy only in part; but when the complete comes, the partial will come to an end. When I was a child, I spoke like a child, I thought like a child, I reasoned like a child; when I became an adult, I put an end to childish ways. For now we see in a mirror, dimly, but then we will see face to face. Now I know only in part; then I will know fully, even as I have been fully known. And now faith, hope, and love abide, these three; and the greatest of these is love.

We know, instinctively, that those words come from the very heart of God. We know that nothing more need be said.

A Final Word

As I greeted people at the door, following that last sermon, it was evident that the words of 1 Corinthians 13 had struck home. People responded with unusual warmth. There was, however, an exception. A visitor to the church who had been a part of an earlier demonstration out front had come into the church to hear the sermon and see what was going on. As she came through the line, she took my hand, looked at me sternly, and said, "That is the worst drivel I have ever heard." Some around her were offended. But I thought, No, she's probably right! Even the best we can do in the pulpit—and rarely do we do our best—must seem like drivel in the eternal perspective of God. Which of our words can even stand the test of human historical time, in the light of which our spiritual limitations and cultural biases will be all too evident?

Still, if we seek to be faithful to the gospel and open to grace and truth, even our drivel can be a part of the word of God to a broken world.